FOR NELSON MANDELA

·F·O·R·

NELSON
MANDELA

EDITED BY

JACQUES DERRIDA
MUSTAPHA TLILI

SEAVER BOOKS

Henry Holt and Company ▲ New York

Published by Seaver Books/Henry Holt and Company, Inc.,
521 Fifth Avenue, New York, New York 10175

Published in Canada by Fitzhenry & Whiteside Limited,
195 Allstate Parkway, Markham, Ontario L3R 4T8

18217406

ISBN 0-8050-0581-1

Library of Congress Cataloging-in-Publication Data
For Nelson Mandela.
"Portions of this book were originally published
in France by Editions Gallimard under the title
Pour Nelson Mandela"—T.p. verso.
1. Apartheid—South Africa—Literary collections.
2. Mandela, Nelson, 1918– —Literary collections.
3. Literature, Modern—20th century—Translations into English.
4. English literature—Translations from foreign languages.
5. English literature—20th century.
I. Mandela, Nelson, 1918– . II. Derrida, Jacques. III. Tlili,
Mustapha, 1937– . IV. Title: Pour Nelson Mandela.
PN6071.A77F67 1987   808.8'0358   87-14379
ISBN: 0-8050-0581-1

First Edition

Designed by Ann Gold
Printed in the United States of America
1 3 5 7 9 10 8 6 4 2

CONTENTS

▼

THE MEANING OF AN ACT OF COMPASSION AND RIGOR: PREFACE TO THE AMERICAN EDITION
by Mustapha Tlili

▼▼

The foreword by Dominique Lecoq* to the French edition of this collective tribute to Nelson Mandela mentions that the project originated in a conversation with Mustapha Tlili. Perhaps it is the genesis of a work of art—and that is what this book aspires to—that best sheds light on its meaning and purpose. So it seems appropriate at the time of the American edition to recall its history and shaping conception.

A few years ago—in 1981—the French painter Ernest Pignon-Ernest and the Spanish Antonio Saura joined with me in setting up an international art exhibition in protest against apartheid. Its goal was a heightening of general awareness of the wrongs of this systematic negation of human rights, but in a manner conducive to reflection and deliberation, thereby to win the undivided support of all people of goodwill to the cause of freedom.

Eighty-five of the most eminent artists of our time responded to the call. Among the American contributors were Arman, Sol Lewitt, Roy Lichtenstein, Robert Motherwell, Claës

---

*French journalist and specialist in African affairs, he assumed the secretarial duties for the project with an effectiveness and selflessness that deserve our warmest thanks.

Oldenburg, Robert Rauschenberg, Larry Rivers, and Saul Steinberg.

Not all the works exhibited directly treat the theme of apartheid or even that of racial discrimination. The artists solicited were free to do as they wished, our only demand being high quality. We had complete confidence in the artists' consciousness of both the dignity of their art and the seriousness of the occasion. We were not disappointed. The collection is destined, at the end of its tour, to constitute a museum to be offered to the first South African government elected by universal suffrage.

The exhibition opened in Paris in November 1983, and thanks to the dynamism of its capable managers, Chantal Bonnet and Sheila Bourne, has since been making its way around the globe, moving with unfailing popularity from one great museum to another—in Finland, Sweden, Denmark, the Federal Republic of Germany, Spain, Greece. And tomorrow, Japan. Everywhere, it has stimulated tens of thousands of visitors—coming in search of esthetic emotions, without preconceived ideas, to an artistic display—to reflect on the intolerable situation existing in South Africa.

The idea of a book honoring Nelson Mandela represents a logical extension of the ideas behind the exhibition. It originated in a dialogue between Antonio Saura, Jacques Derrida, and me during our congenial, enthusiastic collaboration on the exhibition catalogue. So Nelson Mandela has brought us together in yet another enterprise, and another project for furthering freedom, the only meaningful activity for a true creator.

Nelson Mandela is an exceptional political prisoner meriting an exceptional tribute—a literary monument not to the glory of the man, but to the moral figure he has year by year become. A tribute in the way that Plato invoked the memory and presence of Socrates. It matters little, ultimately, whether Socrates was a real individual. He is the Great Witness, and that is the critical thing; just as Gandhi and Martin Luther

King, Jr., are witnesses of our own time.

Yesterday, Socrates faced his judges the Sophists, and engaged in a dialogue with the oppressor. Today, Mandela is the inflexible symbol, and in turn upholds the beacon of a certain idea of humanity and freedom. The ideal for which he struggles includes, despite themselves, the South African whites. Mandela puts the question to us all. He remains the truth of Western law, and the proof of its denial. He is, simply, the harbinger of the Law.

Here you will find no slogan, proclamation, declaration, or anything like a cult of personality. The goal was to gather literary acts of compassion and rigor controlled only by each writer's art and creativity. In plainer language, the book envisioned was to be an ensemble that was strictly ordered around apartheid and/or the experience of Nelson Mandela. Autonomous, coherent pieces, most previously unpublished—and inspired by the authentic writer's necessary values of goodness, beauty, and truth—join voices in harmony to pay tribute to the world's most famous political prisoner. Hence this book was no place for direct, specific political advocacy, however well intentioned. In short, the goal was to be, for a writer in 1987, worthy of the honor of honoring Nelson Mandela.

The texts solicited were also from different genres, and so, we think, avoid didacticism or repetitiveness and arouse emotion.

The result is in the reader's hands. Art, creation, literature in honor of an outstanding figure in human history: the international cast of writers brought together in this book is like a group of close friends reunited for a spell of passionate discourse and conviviality. Each in his or her own way, each with a particular voice—one with rigor, another with metaphors—through the philosophical or political essay, the poem, the novella, the novel, the play, invokes the presence of a wonderful, absent friend and modern conscience, Nelson Mandela. We all admire him, and we all try to convey our admiration to the reader of today or of tomorrow. Why? So one people's struggle against degradation may never be forgotten, but remain a cause for reflection and inspiration for generations.

Have we succeeded? The reader will judge.

Translated from the French by Franklin Philip

FOREWORD TO THE
FRENCH EDITION IN 1985
by Dominique Lecoq

▼▼

Africa now wears the face of Nelson Mandela, which his imprisonment has made changeless. In their attempted use of time to obliterate the man, the racists have succeeded only in giving him a permanent place in history. Africa now wears the face of Nelson Mandela, who chose to remain behind bars rather than accept a conditional release that would not bring true freedom to him and his African brothers. The holder of the absurd, appalling record of being the world's longest-held political prisoner, Mandela has secured his realm, becoming, in a prison cell, the symbol of supreme freedom—not any freedom his jailers could grant, but the freedom sought and secured in struggle, and mingled with life itself. Mandela made Robben Island—that barren rock lost in the ocean and where he was long held—the locus of a confrontation between life and death, making a bet on the dignity of all against a people who, as Jean Paulhan says, are "sensitive to the freedoms that only cast others into a like servitude."

His people have heard the man who struggles to bring the South African nightmare, begun more than fifty years ago in the German nightmare, to an end. For the sake of "human dignity," Mandela would add, for his struggle is not a partisan fight, but calls for a respect for the only valid human law, which recognizes, across time and space, the unity of mankind. Outside this law lies savagery. It is a struggle for dignity, and also against silence.

A friend of mine who escaped after years of confinement in a

South African prison has said that the political prisoner's main need is to know he is not forgotten. To satisfy this, one must jog the memory forgetful of names and words like "apartheid," which is untranslatable into any other language. On what pretext does it cover up the intolerable, through constant repetition, sometimes permitting the same people who give concrete support to the system to condemn it? For the reality of apartheid is concrete—insane in its dailiness—and the South African people alone can change it. Alone does not mean all alone. That is the imperative reason for the existence of this book.

For Nelson Mandela is not a collection of texts centered on a passing topic, but literature, connected, as always, with evil and with death. In his last book Henri Michaux wrote, "He who leaves a trace leaves a wound."

Doubtless the writer must leave a trace of some wound—at this time, an open wound made by the producers of apartheid—not just to stir the forgetful memory, but also, since memory corrupts the meaning of words, to reassert the wound's truth. So it will be a matter of love. In the face of the intolerable, its expression often comes under the heading of a howl of pain or, more reflectively, the bearing of witness. What follows is neither of these, but a trace of the imperious necessity of writing, and of an essential passion for the written word so that the unnameable finally is named. A bet always lost, always played again. The greatest works of literature are born of the desperate attempt to achieve the impossible. These texts answer in this way a question that cannot be explicitly asked, an enigma—the persistence of apartheid despite all remains one of the enigmas of our time—that, say what you will, secretly torments the forms and discourse of contemporary culture.

Originating in a discussion with Mustapha Tlili, and subsequently deliberated over many times, this book was put together from the responses to the invitation that Jacques Derrida and I sent to writers to participate in its writing. The bond was sealed, as if by itself, around the exceptional personality of Nelson Mandela and the original Africa he symbolizes through his particular demand for freedom. An international committee for support was formed, with members from every continent. Besides Jacques Derrida, its members are Adonis, Ba Jin, André Brink, Marguerite Duras, Nadine Gordimer, Michel Leiris, Heiner Müller, Octavio Paz, Susan Sontag, and Wole Soyinka—poets, philosophers, writers.

It was not the goal of this undertaking to get the writers to join in an antiapartheid manifesto—in the face of the humanly intolerable, there can be no alternate choice that any such advocacy would have to weigh. Rather, each was to contribute, according to his or her lights, an original text for a Festschrift to be offered to Nelson Mandela. The space, left free in approach and open to the greatest variety of forms, is now filled with poetry (Adonis, Edmond Jabès, Severo Sarduy), fiction (Olympe Bhêly-Quênum, Hélène Cixous, Nadine Gordimer, Mustapha Tlili), essays (Jorge Amado, Maurice Blanchot, Jacques Derrida, Juan Goytisolo, Heiner Müller, Susan Sontag), and drama (Kateb Yacine).

Other writers, such as Salman Rushdie and Christa Wolf, hailed the effort without being able to take part themselves. For Nelson Mandela is an event that, thanks to the diversity and caliber of its contributors, has no precedent in the history of literature.

Lodged in this book, in a certain way, is the solution to the enigma which, in the end, carries the day and remains unchanged. Nevertheless, something will have changed, like a subtle deepening of conviction: apartheid will have one face, and freedom another that restores Africa to its universal calling. Freedom will henceforth wear the face of Nelson Mandela.

Translated from the French by Franklin Philip

NADINE GORDIMER

NELSON MANDELA:
A TRIBUTE

▽

Nelson Mandela has been in prison since June 1964. For more than twenty years his speeches and writings have been banned in South Africa; neither his voice nor his words have reached his people. When his photograph appears in newspapers it is the image of a man many years younger than the living man.

A whole generation has been born and grown up while he has been incarcerated, first on the prison island off Cape Town, then in a mainland prison. Yet there is no black child in whose face, at the mention of his name, there is not instant recognition. And there are few whites, young and old—enemies of the cause of black freedom as well as its supporters—who do not know who this man is.

Nelson Mandela is *there,* in South Africa. His body has been hidden behind walls; his presence has never been obliterated by them. His people have never revered him as a figure of the past, but as *the* personification of the future, which could not be contained by the moat of the Atlantic Ocean around Robben Island and cannot be contained by the "maximum security" of any other prison in the land. His name is part of everyday talk, it is invoked wherever people meet to resist racism and oppression, it is sung and chanted to . . . to give strength in sorrow and to express heart in celebration. When Bishop Desmond Tutu received the Nobel Peace Prize in the twentieth year of Mandela's imprisonment, he said that he

3

accepted it for Mandela, for all prisoners of conscience, and for all those ordinary black people whose employers do not even know their workers' surnames. To those ordinary people, whether or not they support the African National Congress, Nelson Mandela is the man of every year. If Mandela were to be released in 1985 to take the place he has kept among us, he would bring with him our last hope of a peaceful end to apartheid.

EXCERPT FROM
BURGER'S DAUGHTER

▼

She didn't live in an official township at all but in one of those undefined areas between black men's hostels and the mine dumps on the outskirts of the city. Small industries have taken over the property of worked-out gold mines, the hollows are mass graves for wrecked cars and machine parts, the old pepper trees are shade for shebeens, and prostitutes lie down for customers in the sand of the dumps. There were still hawkers' mules tethered in grazed circumferences of tin-littered veld; a tiny corrugated-iron church with broken windows, and a peach tree half hacked away for firewood; in abandoned cottages that had once belonged to white miners, and in the yards built up with shelters made of materials gathered from the bulldozed mine compounds and the brick shells of concession stores, people were living in what had been condemned and abandoned by the white city. This was the "place"; she assured me it would do to stop anywhere on the switchback I was driving between dongas and boulders of the tracks that bound bricks, tin, and smoke. God would bless me: with this she went off with her stolid side-to-side gait through bicycles and listing taxis hooting at her. Perhaps she didn't really live there—she looked much too respectable for this sort of den existing on the sale of sex and drink to factory workers and railway yard laborers. It's impossible to say; for Flora's white women to imagine where on earth they come from, these neat black ladies they meet in Flora's house. Prob-

ably the old mother thought she'd take advantage of the pro-
vision of car and driver and go and visit an out-of-the-way
friend—why not?

I was miles from where Marisa lived, from where I could
go to her cousin Fats' place and send someone to see if I
could slip into her house by way of yards. I wasn't even sure
how to get across to the township without going all the way
back through town. There was a woman with a tin of live
coal, selling roast mealies, and I got out of the car to go over
and ask directions of her. She didn't know. Orlando might
have been at the other end of the world. The ribbed papery
husks stripped from cobs made a thick mat all round her,
under the soles of my shoes as it was under bare feet when
Tony, the other Marie, and I pranced with black farm kids
around the thresher on Uncle Coen's farm. I made for a gang
of black children and youths now, the little ones dancing and
jumping among excited dogs to touch a bike with ram's-horn
racing handles, a young chap astride it in the center of other
adolescents sharing smokes and a half-jack of something
wrapped in brown paper. I called to them but they only cat-
called and laughed back in wolf-whistle falsetto. I was approaching—smiling, no, be serious for a moment, tell me—I
heard the hard ring of struck metal and saw the fall of a stone
that had hit my old car. I drove away while they went on
laughing and yelling as if I were at once prey and a girl for
teasing. I took wheel-tracks deep enough to be well used that
seemed to lead over the veld to a road away on the rise in the
right direction. The hump of dead grass down the middle
swished against the belly of the car and now and then the oil-
sump scraped hard earth. The track went on and on. I was
caught on the countersystem of communications that doesn't
appear on the road maps and provides access to "places" that
don't appear on any plan of city environs. I was obstinate,
sure the track would be crossed by one that led to the main
road somewhere; there was a cemetery half a kilometer across
the veld with the hired buses as prominent as sudden buildings, and the mass of black people and black umbrellas like

the heap of some dark crop standing on the pale open veld, that mark a Saturday funeral. I gained a cambered dirt road without signposts just as one of those donkey carts that survive on the routes between these places that don't exist was approaching along a track from the opposite side. Driver's reflex made me slow down in anticipation that the cart might turn in up ahead without calculating the speed of an oncoming car. But there was something strange about the outline of donkey, cart, and driver; convulsed, yet the cart was not coming nearer. As I drew close I saw a woman and child bundled under sacks, their heads jerked rocking; a driver standing up on the cart in a wildly precarious spread of legs in torn pants. Suddenly his body arched back with one upflung arm against the sky and lurched over as if he had been shot and at that instant the donkey was bowed by a paroxysm that seemed to draw its four legs and head down toward the center of its body in a noose, then flung head and extremities wide again; and again the man violently salaamed, and again the beast curved together and flew apart.

I didn't see the whip. I saw agony. Agony that came from some terrible center seized within the group of donkey, cart, driver, and people behind him. They made a single object that contracted against itself in the desperation of a hideous final energy. Not seeing the whip, I saw the infliction of pain broken away from the will that creates it; broken loose, a force existing of itself, ravishment without the ravisher, torture without the torturer, rampage, pure cruelty gone beyond control of the humans who have spent thousands of years devising it. The entire ingenuity from thumbscrew and rack to electric shock, the infinite variety and gradation of suffering, by lash, by fear, by hunger, by solitary confinement—the camps, concentration, labor, resettlement, the Siberias of snow or sun, the lives of Mandela, Sisulu, Mbeki, Kathrada, Kgosana, gull-picked on the Island, Lionel propped wasting to his skull between two warders, the deaths by questioning, bodies fallen from the height of John Vorster Square, deaths by dehydration, babies degutted by enteritis in "places" of banishment, the lights beating all night on faces of those in cells—Conrad—I conjure you up, I drag you back from wherever you are to listen to me—you don't know what I saw, what there is to see, you *won't* see, you are becalmed on an empty ocean.

Only when I was level with the cart, across the veld from me, did I make out the whip. The donkey didn't cry out. Why didn't the donkey give that bestial snort and squeal of excruciation I've heard donkeys give not in pain but in rut? It didn't cry out.

It had been beaten and beaten. Pain was no shock, there is no way out of the shafts. That rag of a black man was old, from the stance of his legs, the scraggle of beard showing under an old hat in a shapeless cone over his face. I rolled to a stop beyond what I saw; the car simply fell away from the pressure of my foot and carried me no farther. I sat there with my head turned sharply and my shoulders hunched around my neck, huddled to my ears against the blows. And then I put my foot down and drove on wavering drunkenly about the road, pausing to gaze back while the beating still went on, the force there, cart, terrified woman and child, the donkey and man, bucked and bolted zigzag under the whip. I had only to turn the car in the empty road and drive up upon that mad frieze against the sunset putting out my eyes. When I looked over there all I could see was the writhing black shape through whose interstices poked searchlights of blinding bright dust. The thing was like an explosion. I had only to career down on that scene with my car and my white authority. I could have yelled before I even got out, yelled to stop!—and then there I would have been standing, inescapable, fury and right, might, before them, the frightened woman and child and the drunk, brutal man, with my knowledge of how to deliver them over to the police, to have him prosecuted as he deserved and should be, to take away from him the poor suffering possession he maltreated. I could formulate everything they were, as the act I had witnessed; they would have their lives summed up for them officially at last by me, the white woman—the final meaning of a day they had lived I had no knowledge of, a day of other appalling things, violence, disasters, urgencies, deprivations which suddenly would become, was nothing but what it had led up to: the man among them beating their donkey. I could have put a stop to it, the misery; at that point I witnessed. What more can one do? That sort of old man, those people, peasants existing the only way they know how in the "place" that isn't on the map, they would have been afraid of me. I could have put a stop to it, with them, at no risk to myself. No one would have taken up a stone. I was safe from the whip. I could have stood between them and suffering—the suffering of the donkey.

As soon as I planted myself in front of them it would have become again just that—the pain of a donkey.

I drove on. I don't know at what point to intercede makes sense, for me. Every week the woman who comes to clean my flat and wash my clothes brings a child whose make-believe is polishing floors and doing washing. I drove on because the horrible drunk was black, poor, and brutalized. If somebody's going to be brought to account, I am accountable for him, to him, as he is for the donkey. Yet the suffering—while I saw it it was the sum of suffering to me. I didn't do anything. I let him beat the donkey. The man was a black. So a kind of vanity counted for more than feeling; I couldn't bear to see myself—her—Rosa Burger—as one of those whites who can care more for animals than people. Since I've been free, I'm free to become one.

I went without saying good-bye to Marisa.

Someone threw a stone, yes. Perhaps one of the little ones with baby brothers or sisters humped on their backs, shouting *voetsak!* at the dogs, flung a stone not meant for me. If someone did report I'd been at a public meeting with a possible political intention, there were no consequences. Nothing and nobody stopped me from using that passport. After the donkey I couldn't stop myself. I don't know how to live in Lionel's country.

JACQUES
DERRIDA

THE LAWS OF REFLECTION:
NELSON MANDELA, IN ADMIRATION

▼▼

1

Admirable Mandela.

Period, no exclamation point. I am not using this punctuation to temper any enthusiasm or to be a killjoy. Instead of speaking only in honor of Nelson Mandela, I shall say something about his honor without succumbing, if possible, to loftiness, without proclaiming or acclaiming.

The homage will perhaps be more exact, as will its tone, if it seems to surrender its impatience, without which there would be no question of admiring, to the coldness of an analysis. Admiration reasons, whatever is said of it, it works things out with reason, it astonishes and interrogates: how can one be Mandela? Why does he seem exemplary and admirable in what he thinks and says, in what he does or in what he suffers? Admirable in himself, as well as in what he conveys as a witness, another word for martyrdom, that is to say the experience of his people?

"My people and I," he always says, without speaking like a king.

Why does he also *force* admiration in this manner? This word presupposes some resistance, for his enemies admire him without admitting it. Unlike those who love him among his people and together with his inseparable Winnie, from whom these enemies have always futilely kept him separated,

these enemies fear him. If his most hateful persecutors secretly admire him, this proves that, as one might say, he forces
such admiration.

So, this is the question: where does that force come from?
Where does it lead? It is used or is applied, but for what? Or
rather: what *folds* under it? What form is to be recognized in
this fold? What line?

First of all we will see in it, and let's say it without any
other premise, *the line of a reflection*. This is first of all a force
of reflection. What is obvious right away is that Mandela's
political experience or passion can never be separated from a
theoretical reflection: about history, culture, and above all
jurisprudence. An unremitting analysis enlightens the rational-
ity of his acts, his demonstrations, his speeches, his strategy.
Even before being constrained to withdraw from the world
into prison, and during a quarter of a century of incarcera-
tion, he has been acting endlessly and giving a direction to
the struggle. Mandela has always been, like all the greatest
politicians, a man of reflection.

But by force of reflection, something else can be understood, beckoning toward the literality of the mirror and the
scene of specularity/speculation. Not so much toward the
physical laws of reflection as toward specular paradoxes in
the experience of the law. There is no law without a mirror.
And in this properly reversible structure, we shall never avoid
the moment of admiration.

Admiration, as its name indicates, it will be said, etc. No,
no matter what its name or that it always enables us to *see*,
admiration does not just belong to sight. It translates emotion,
astonishment, surprise, interrogation in the face of that which
oversteps the mark: in the face of the "extraordinary," says
Descartes, and he considers it a passion, the first of the six
primitive passions, before love, hate, desire, joy, and sadness.
It enables understanding. Outside of it there is only ignorance,
he adds, and in it resides "a great deal of force" of "surprise"
or of "sudden arrival." The admiring look is astonished, it
questions its intuition, it opens upon the light of a question

but of a question received no less than asked. This experience lets the light of a question pass through it, which in no way prevents it from reflecting it. The light has as focus the very thing which forces admiration, it partitions it then into a specular movement which seems strangely fascinating.

Mandela becomes admirable for having known how to admire. And what he has discovered, he has found through admiration. He fascinates too, as we shall see, for having been fascinated.

That, in a certain way which we will have to understand, is what *he says*. He states what he does and what has happened to him. Such a light, its reflected passage, as experience of the give-and-take of a question would thus also be the burst of a voice.

Nelson Mandela's voice—what does it remind us of, ask from us, demand of us? I mean to say what do the dynamics of that voice have to do with sight, reflection, admiration, but also what sings in his name? (Listen to the clamor of his people when they demonstrate in his name: Man-de-la!)

Admiration of Nelson Mandela, as we might say Nelson Mandela's passion. Admiration of Mandela, a double genitive: the one he inspires and the one he feels. The two have the same focus, they reflect upon each other. I have already stated my hypothesis: he becomes admirable for having, with all his force, admired, and for having made a force of his admiration, a combative, untreatable, and irreducible power. The law itself, the law above other laws.

For in fact what has he admired? In one word: the Law. And what inscribes it in discourse, in history, in the institution is jurisprudence.

A first quotation—a lawyer is speaking, during a trial, his trial, the one where he is also prosecuting, the one in which he prosecutes those who accuse him, in the name of the law:

> The basic task at the present moment is the removal of race discrimination and the attainment of democratic rights on the basis of the Freedom Charter. . . . From my reading of

Marxist literature and from conversations with Marxists, I have gained the impression that communists regard the parliamentary system of the West as undemocratic and reactionary. But, on the contrary, *I am an admirer* of such a system. The *Magna Charta*, the Petition of Rights, and the Bill of Rights are documents which are held in veneration by democrats throughout the world. *I have great respect* for British political institutions, and for the country's system of justice. I regard the British Parliament as the most democratic institution in the world, and the independence and impartiality of its judiciary never fail to arouse my admiration.[1]

He admires the law, he says it clearly, but is this law, which gives orders to constitutions and declarations, essentially a thing of the West? Does its formal universality retain some irreducible link with European history, even with an Anglo-American one? If it were so, we would of course still have to meditate upon this strange possibility: that its formal character would be as essential to the universality of the law as its presentation in a determined moment and place in history. How could we conceive of such a history? The struggle against apartheid, wherever it takes place and such as Mandela carries it on and reflects it, would this remain a sort of specular opposition, a domestic war that the West carried on with itself, in its own name? An internal contradiction which would not put up with either a radical otherness or a true dissymmetry?

In this form, such a hypothesis still implies too many indistinct presuppositions. We shall try to recognize them later. For the moment, let's retain an obvious, more limited but also more certain fact: what Mandela admires and says he admires is the tradition inaugurated by the Magna Charta, the Univer-

1. Nelson Mandela, *The Struggle Is My Life* (London: International Defence and Aid for Southern Africa, 1978), p. 170. All the following quotes are taken from this publication and the italicized words are Jacques Derrida's.

sal Declaration of the Rights of Man under their diverse forms (he frequently calls upon "human dignity," upon what is human and "worthy of that name"); it's also parliamentary democracy and, still more precisely, the doctrine of the separation of powers, the independence of justice.

But if he admires this tradition, does it mean that he is its inheritor, its simple inheritor? Yes and no, depending on what is meant here by inheritance. You can recognize an authentic inheritor in the one who conserves and reproduces, but also in the one who respects the *logic* of the legacy enough to turn it upon occasion against those who claim to be its guardians, enough to reveal, despite and against the usurpers, what has never yet been seen in the inheritance: enough to give birth, by the unheard-of *act* of a reflection, to what had never seen the light of day.

2

This inflexible logic of reflection was also Mandela's practice. Here are at least two signs of it.

1. *First sign.* The African National Congress, of which he was one of the leaders after having joined it in 1944, succeeded the South African National Congress. Now the structure of the latter already reflected that of the American Congress and the House of Lords. It included in particular a High Chamber. The paradigm was then already this parliamentary democracy Mandela admired. The Charter of Freedom, which he promulgated in 1955, also enunciates those democratic principles inspired by the Universal Declaration of the Rights of Man. And yet, with an exemplary rigor, Mandela nonetheless refuses pure and simple alliance with the liberal whites who wanted to maintain the struggle within the constitutional framework, such at least as it was then established. Mandela reminds us, in fact, of the truth: the establishment of this constitutional law had not only, both in fact and in practice, taken the form of a singular coup de force, but this violent act *at once* produced *and* presupposed the unity of a nation. In this case, the

coup de force *remained* a coup de force, thus, as a bad coup—
a bad blow—and the failure of a law that never managed to
establish itself. It always had, in fact, for its authors and ben-
efactors, only a particular will, that of a part of the population, a limited sum of private interests, those of the white
minority. The latter becomes the privileged subject, the only
subject in truth of this anticonstitutional constitution. It is
probable, as it might be said, that such a coup de force always
marks the founding of a nation, state, or nation-state. In the
event of such a founding or institution, the properly *performative* act must produce (proclaim) what in the form of a
constative act it merely claims, declares, assures it is describing. The simulacrum or fiction then consists in bringing to
daylight, *in giving birth to,* that which one claims to reflect so
as to take note of it, as though it were a matter of recording
what *will have been there,* the unity of a nation, the founding
of a state, while one is in the act of producing that event. But
legitimacy, indeed legality, becomes permanently installed, it
recovers its originating violence, and is forgotten only under
certain conditions. Not all performatives, a theoretician of
speech acts would say, are "happy." That depends on a great
number of conditions and conventions that form the context
of such events. In the case of South Africa, certain "conventions" were not respected, the violence was too great, *visibly
too great,* at a moment when this visibility extended to a new
international scene, and so on. The white community was *too*
much in the minority, the disproportion of wealth *too* flagrant.
From then on this violence remains at once excessive and
powerless, insufficient in its result, lost in its own contradiction. It cannot manage to have itself forgotten, as in the case
of states founded on a genocide or a quasi-extermination.
Here, the violence of the origin must repeat itself indefinitely
and act out its rightfulness in a legislative apparatus whose
monstrosity fails to pay back: a pathological proliferation of
juridical prostheses (laws, acts, amendments) destined to le-
galize to the slightest detail the effects of fundamental racism,
of a state racism, the unique and the last in the world.

The constitution of such a state cannot then, even with a sufficient verisimilitude, refer back to the popular will. As the Charter of Liberty reminds us: "South Africa belongs to all its inhabitants, black and white. No government can prevail over an authority which isn't founded on the will of the entire nation." Referring to the general will, which cannot be reduced to the sum of the wills of the "entire nation," Mandela often reminds us of Rousseau even if he never quotes him. And he thus contests the authority, the legality, the constitutionality of the Constitution. He thus refuses the proposal of—and the alliance with—the white liberals who would struggle against apartheid even as they claim to respect the legal framework:

> The credo of the liberals consists in "the use of democratic and constitutional means, rejecting the several forms of totalitarianism: fascism and communism." Only a people already enjoying democratic and constitutional rights has any grounds for speaking of democratic and constitutional rights. This does not have any meaning for those who do not benefit from them.[2]

What does Mandela oppose to the coup de force of the white minority which has instituted a supposedly democratic law, but a law which in fact benefits only a single ethnonational entity? The "entire nation," that is to say another ethnonational entity, another collectivity formed of all the groups, including the white minority, inhabiting the territory named South Africa. This other entity could not have instituted, nor in the future will be able to institute, itself as the subject of the State of the Constitution of South Africa except by a performative act. And the performative will not appear to

2. Translators' note: The translation of this quote is ours; Jacques Derrida takes it from the French introduction and its source is unclear; Nelson Mandela, *L'Apartheid,* préface de Breyten Breytenbach (Paris, Les Editions de Minuit, 1985), p. 19. A comparative reading can be obtained for all the following Mandela quotes from the French mentioned above.

refer to any fundamental preexisting law, only to the "convention" of geographic and demographic delimitation effected, in large measure, by white colonization. This fact remains ineffaceable. No doubt the will of the "entire nation," in any case the general will, should erase itself from all empirical determination. Such is at least its regulating ideal. It seems no more accessible here than anywhere else. The definition of the "entire nation" registers—and thus seems to reflect—the event of the coup de force that white occupation, followed by the founding of the South African Republic, was. Without this event, how could we recognize the slightest relationship between a general will and what the Charter of Freedom calls the "will of the entire nation"? The latter finds itself paradoxically united by the violence done to it, which tends to disintegrate or to destructure it forever, in its more virtual identity. This phenomenon marks the establishment of almost all states after a decolonization. Mandela knows that: no matter how democratic it is, and even if it seems to conform to the principle of the equality of all before the law, the absolute inauguration of a state cannot presuppose the previously *legitimized* existence of a national entity. The same is true for a first constitution. The total unity of a nation is not identified for the first time except by a contract—formal or not, written or not—which institutes some fundamental law. Now this contract is never actually signed, except by supposed representatives of the nation which is supposed to be "entire." This fundamental law cannot, either in law or in fact, simply precede that which at once institutes it and nevertheless supposes it: projecting and reflecting it! It can in no way precede this extraordinary performative by which a signature authorizes itself to sign, in a word, legalizes itself on its own without the guarantee of a preexisting law. This violence and this autographic fiction are found at work just as surely in what we call individual autobiography as in the "historical" origin of states. In the case of South Africa, the fiction lies in this—and it is a fiction against a fiction: the unity of the "entire nation" could not correspond to the delimitation effected by the white minority. It should now constitute a whole (the white minority plus all the inhabitants of South Africa) whose configuration was only able to be established, in any case to be identified, by beginning with a minority violence. That it can from then on oppose this violence alters nothing about this terrifying contradiction. The "entire nation," a unity of "all the national groups," will grant itself existence and legal force only by the very same act to which the Charter of Freedom appeals. This Charter speaks in the present, a present supposed to be founded on the *description* of a historical fact, which, in turn, should be recognized in the future. It also speaks in the future, a future which has *prescriptive* value:

> South Africa belongs to all its inhabitants, black and white. No government can claim an authority which is not founded on the will of the entire people.
> —The people will govern.
> —All the national groups will enjoy equal rights. . . .
> —All will be equal before the law.[3]

The Charter does not annul the founding act of the law, this act necessarily alegal in itself, which finally institutes South Africa and can only become legal after the fact, notably if it is ratified by the right of the international community. No, the Charter refounds it, or in any case intends to refound it, by *reflecting* against the white minority the principles from which it was claiming to be inspired, whereas *actually* it never ceased to betray them. A democracy, yes, South Africa yes, but this time, says the Charter, the "entire nation" must include all the national groups, such is the very logic of the law to which the white minority was pretending to appeal. Upon this territory so marked out, all human beings, all the people "worthy of this name," will thus become effectively the subjects of the law.

2. *Second sign.* The "admiration" declared for the model of

3. Translators' note: Translation is ours; pp. 19–20 in the French publication.

parliamentary democracy of the Anglo-American type and for the separation of powers, the faithfulness of the Charter to all the principles of such a democracy, the logic of a radicalization which opposes these very principles to the Western defenders of apartheid, all of this could be seen to resemble the coup de force of a simple specular inversion: the struggle of the black community (or non-"white" communities) would be undertaken in the name of an imported law and model, which were betrayed, in the first place, by the first to import them. A terrifying dissymmetry. But it seems to reduce itself, or rather, to reflect itself to the point of withdrawing from every objective representation: neither symmetry nor dissymmetry. And this because there would be no importation, no simply assignable origin for the history of law, only a reflecting apparatus, with projections of images, inversions of paths, interior duplications, and effects of history for a law whose structure and whose "history" consist in taking away the origin. Such an apparatus, and by this word I only mean that this *x* is not natural (which does not necessarily define it as an artifact brought forth from human hands), cannot be represented in objective space. For at least *two reasons* that I shall here relate to the case that occupies us.

The first reason concerns the structure of the law, of the principle or model being considered. Whatever the historical place of its formation or formulation, of its revelation or presentation, a structure of this kind tends toward universality. Here we have, as it were, its intentional content; its meaning requires that in its immediacy it must extend beyond the historical, national, geographical, linguistic, and cultural limits of its phenomenal origin. Everything should begin by uprooting. The limits would then appear to be empirical contingencies. They could even dissimulate what they seem to show. Thus one might think that the "white minority" of South Africa is hiding the essence of the principles to which it claims to be appealing, it is privatizing them, particularizing them, appropriating them, and in that way taking them over against their very reason for being, against reason itself. Whereas, in the struggle against apartheid, the "reflection" of which we are speaking here would make visible what was not even visible any longer in the political phenomenality dominated by the whites. It would oblige us to see what was no longer seen or was not yet to be seen. It tries to open the eyes of the whites; it does not reproduce the visible, it produces it. This reflection makes visible a law that in truth it does more than reflect, because this law, in its phenomenon, was invisible— had become or continued to be invisible. Transporting the invisible into the visible, this reflection does not proceed from the visible, rather it passes through understanding. More exactly, it reveals to understanding what goes past understanding and relates only to reason. It was a first reason, reason itself.

The second reason seems more problematic. It specifically concerns this phenomenal apparition, the historical constitution of the law, of democratic principles and the democratic model. Here again, the experience of declared admiration— this time of an admiration that is said to be *fascinated*—follows the line of a reflection. Still a reflection upon the law: Mandela perceives, he *sees,* others might say that he *projects and reflects without seeing it,* the very presence of this law in the interior of African society. Even before "the arrival of the white man."

In what he himself says about this subject, I will underline three themes:

1. that of *fascination:* the attentiveness of the long stare, petrified, by something that, without being simply a visible object, looks at you, already concerns you, understands you, and orders you to continue observing, responding, making you responsible for the look that looks at you and beckons you beyond the visible: neither perception nor hallucination.

2. that of the *seed:* it furnishes an indispensable scheme for interpretation. It is by its virtuality that the democratic model would have been present in the society of ancestors, even if it was not to be revealed, *developed* as such

for reflection, until afterward, after the violent eruption of the "white man," the bearer of the same model.

3. that of the South African "homeland," the birthplace of all the national groups called upon to live under the law of the new South African Republic. This country is not to be confused either with the state or with the nation:

Many years ago, when I was a boy brought up in my village in the Transkei, I listened to the elders of the tribe telling stories about the good old days, *before the arrival of the white man.* Then our people lived peacefully, under the *democratic* rule of their kings and their *amapakati,* and moved freely and confidently up and down the country without let or hindrance. Then the country was ours. . . . I hoped and vowed then that, among the treasures that life might offer me, would be the opportunity to serve my people and make my own humble contribution to their freedom struggles.

The structure and organization of early African societies in this country *fascinated* me very much and greatly influenced the evolution of my political outlook. The land, then the main means of production, belonged to the whole tribe, and there was no individual ownership whatsoever. There were no classes, no rich or poor, and no exploitation of man by man. All men were free and equal and this was the foundation of government. Recognition of this general principle found expression in the constitution of the council. . . .

There was much in such a society that was primitive and insecure and it certainly could never measure up to the demands of the present epoch. But in such a society are contained *the seeds of a revolutionary democracy* in which none will be held in slavery or servitude, and in which poverty, want, and insecurity shall be no more. . . .

It is common knowledge that the conference decided that, in place of the unilateral proclamation of a Republic by the White minority of South Africans only, it would demand in the name of the African people the calling of a truly national convention representative of all South Africans, irrespective of their color, black and white, to sit amicably round a table, to debate a new constitution for South Africa, which was in essence what the Government was doing by the proclamation of a Republic, and furthermore, to press on behalf of the African people, that such a new constitution should differ from the constitution of the proposed South African Republic by guaranteeing democratic rights on a basis of full equality to all South Africans of adult age. (p. 141)

What fascination seems to bring into view here, what mobilizes and immobilizes Mandela's attention, is not only parliamentary democracy, whose principle would be presented in the West *as an example but not exemplarily*. It is also the *already virtually* accomplished passage, if one can say this, from parliamentary democracy to revolutionary democracy: a society without class and without private property. We have just recognized, then, this supplementary paradox: the *effective* accomplishment, the filling out of the democratic form, the *real* determination of the formality, *will only have taken place* in the past of this non-Western society, under the species of virtuality, in other words, those "seeds." Mandela lets himself be *fascinated* by what he sees being reflected in advance, what is not yet to be seen, what he fore-sees: the really revolutionary democracy of which the Anglo-American West would, in sum, have only given an image at once incomplete, formal, *and thus also potential*. Potentiality against potentiality, power against power. For if he "admires" the parliamentary systems of the most Western West, he also declares his "admiration," and it is still his word, still the same one, for the "structure and organization of early African societies in this country." It is a question of "seed" and of preformation, according to the same logic or the same rhetoric, a sort of genoptics. The figures of African society prefigure, they make visible ahead of time, what still remains invisible in its historical phenomenon, that is to say, the "classless" society and the end of the "exploitation of man by man":

Today I am attracted by the idea of a classless society, an attraction which springs in part from Marxist reading and, in part, from *my admiration* of the structure and organization of early African societies in this country. The land, then the main means of production, belonged to the tribe. There were no rich or poor, and there was no exploitation of man by man. (p. 170)

3

In all the senses of this term, Mandela remains, then, a *man of the law.* He has always appealed to the law even if, in appearance, he has to oppose himself to such-and-such specific legality, and even if certain judges have made of him, at certain moments, an outlaw.

A man of the law, he was this first *by vocation.* On the one hand, he always appeals to law. On the other hand, he has always felt himself attracted by, appealed to by the law before which people have wanted him to appear. He has moreover accepted to appear before it, even if he was also constrained to do so. He seizes the occasion, we don't dare to say, the good opportunity. Why the good opportunity? Let us reread his "defense" which is in truth an indictment. We will find there a political autobiography, his and that of his people, indissociable. The "I" of this autobiography establishes himself and justifies himself, reasons and signs in the name of "we." He always says "my people," as we have already noted, especially when he asks the question of the subject responsible *before the law:*

> I am charged with inciting people to commit an offence by way of protest against the law, a law which neither I nor any of my people had any say in preparing. The law against which the protest was directed is the law which established a Republic in the Union of South Africa. . . . But in weighing up the decision as to the sentence which is to be imposed for such an offence, the Court must take into account the question of responsibility, whether it is I who is responsible or whether, in fact, a large measure of the responsibility does

not lie on the shoulders of the Government which promulgated
that law, knowing that my people, who constitute the majority
of the population of this country, were opposed to that law, and
knowing further that every legal means of demonstrating that
opposition had been closed to them by prior legislation, and by
Government administrative action. (pp. 139–140)

So he presents himself in this way. He presents himself in
his people, before the law. Before a law he rejects, beyond
any doubt, but which he rejects in the name of a superior
law, the very one he declares to admire and before which he
agrees *to appear.* In such a presentation of the self, he justifies
himself in resuming his history, which he reflects in a single
center, a single and double center, his history and that of his
people. Appearance: they appear together, he becomes himself
again appearing before the law that he summons as much as
he is summoned by it. But he does not present himself *in view
of* a justification which would follow his appearance. The presentation of the self is not *in the service* of the law, it is not a
means. The unfolding of this history is a *justification,* it is possible and has meaning only before the law. He is only what
he is, he, Nelson Mandela, he and his people, he has presence
only in this movement of justice.

Memories and confessions of a lawyer. The latter "confesses" in fact, even as he justifies it, even to the point of
claiming it proudly, a fault in the eyes of legality. Taking as
his witness humanity as a whole, he addresses himself to the
universal justice above his judges of one day only. Whence
this paradox: we can perceive a sort of joyous quivering
throughout the tale of this martyrdom. And sometimes we
think we hear Rousseau's accent in these confessions, hearing
a voice which never ceases to appeal to *the voice of conscience,*
to the immediate and unfailing sentiment of justice, to this
law of laws that speaks in us before us, because it is inscribed
within our heart. In the same tradition, it is also the place of
a categorical imperative, of a morality incommensurate with

the conditional hypotheses and strategies of self-interest, as it is with the figures of such-and-such civil law:

> I do not believe, Your Worship, that this Court, in inflicting penalties on me for the crimes for which I am convicted, should be moved by the belief that penalties deter men from the course that they believe is right. History shows that penalties do not deter men when their *conscience* is aroused. . . . (p. 150)

> Whatever sentence Your Worship sees fit to impose upon me for the crime for which I have been convicted before this Court, may it rest assured that when my sentence has been completed, I will still be moved, as men are always moved, by their *consciences;* I will still be moved by my dislike of the race discrimination against my people when I come out from serving my sentence, to take up again, as best I can, the struggle for the removal of those injustices until they are finally abolished once and for all. (p. 151)

> It was an act of defiance of the law. We were aware that it was, but, nevertheless, that act had been forced on us against our wishes, and we could do no other than to choose between compliance with the law and compliance with our *consciences.* (p. 143)

> [We] were faced with this *conflict between the law and our conscience.* In the face of the complete failure of the Government to heed, to consider, or even to respond to our seriously proposed objections and our solutions to the forthcoming Republic, what were we to do? Were we to allow the law, which states that you shall not commit an offence by way of protest, to take its course and thus betray our *conscience?* . . . In such a dilemma, men of honesty, men of purpose, and men of public morality and of conscience can only have one answer. They must *follow the dictate of their conscience* irrespective of the consequences which might overtake them for it. We of the Action Council, and I particularly, as secretary, *followed our conscience.* (p. 145)

Conscience and conscience of the law, these two make only one. Presentation of oneself and presentation of one's people, these two make only a single history in a single reflection, in both cases, as we have said, a single and double focus. And it is that of admiration, since this conscience presents itself, resumes itself, gathers in reflecting upon itself before the law. That is to say, let's not forget, before what is admirable.

The experience of admiration is also *doubly interior.* It reflects reflection and draws from it all the strength it uses against its Western judges. For it proceeds dramatically, from a double interiorization. Mandela interiorizes also, at the same time, the *principles of interiority* in the figure that the Christian West has given it. All its traits are to be found in the philosophy, the politics, the jurisprudence, and the morality which dominate in Europe: the law of laws resides in the most intimate conscience, we must in the final instance judge intentions and goodwill, and so on. Before any juridical or political discourse, before the texts of positive law, the law speaks by the voice of conscience or is inscribed in the depths of the heart.

A man of law *by vocation,* then, Mandela was that also by profession. It is known that he first studied jurisprudence on the advice of Walter Sisulu, then the Secretary of the National African Council. It was in particular a question of mastering Western law, this weapon to turn against the oppressors. These do not finally realize, in spite of all their legal ruses, the true force of a law that they manipulate, violate, and betray.

To be able to inscribe himself in the system, and above all in the faculty of law, Mandela takes courses by *correspondence.*

He wants to obtain first a degree in letters. Let's stress this episode. Since he cannot have immediate access to direct, personal conversation, he has to begin by correspondence. Mandela will complain about this later. The context, no doubt, will be different, but there will always be a politics of voice and writing, of the difference between what is said "aloud" and what is written, between the "live voice" and "correspondence."

We have been conditioned by the history of White governments in this country to accept the fact that Africans, when
they make their demands strongly and powerfully enough to
have some chance of success, will be met by force and terror
on the part of the Government. This is not something we
have taught the African people, this is something the African
people have learned from their own bitter experience. . . .
Already there are indications in this country that people, my
people, Africans, are turning to deliberate acts of violence
and of force against the Government, in order to persuade
the Government, in the only language which this Government
shows, by its behavior, that it understands.

Elsewhere in the world, a court would say to me, "You
should have made representations to the Government." This
Court, I am confident, will not say so. Representations have
been made, by people who have gone before me, time and
time again. Representations were made in this case by me; I
do not want again to repeat the experience of those representations. The Court cannot expect a respect for the process
of representation and negotiation to grow amongst the African people, when the Government shows every day, by its
conduct, that it despises such processes and frowns upon
them and will not indulge in them. Nor will the Court, I
believe, say that, under the circumstances, my people are
condemned forever to say nothing and to do nothing. (pp.
147–148)

In order not to hear, not to understand, the white Government requires that one writes to it. But it also means thus not
to answer and first of all not to read. Mandela reminds us of
the letter that Albert Luthuli, then the president of the ANC,
had addressed to the first minister Strijdom. It was a lengthy
analysis of the situation, accompanied by a request for a consultation. Not the slightest response.

The standard of behavior of the South African Government
towards my people, and its aspirations, has not always been
what it should have been, and is not always the standard
which is to be expected in serious high-level dealings between

civilized peoples. Chief Luthuli's letter was not even favored
with the courtesy of an acknowledgment from the Prime Minister's office. (p. 144)

The white power does not believe itself required to respond,
does not hold itself responsible before the black people. The
blacks cannot assure themselves, by return mail, by verbal
exchange, by any look or sign, that any image of them has
been formed on the other side, which might afterward return
to it in some way. For the white power does not content itself
with not answering. It does worse: it does not even acknowledge receipt. After Luthuli, Mandela experiences it himself.
He has just written to Verwoerd to inform him of a resolution
voted on by the action committee of which he is then the
secretary. He requests also that a national convention be con-
voked before the deadline determined by the resolution. Neither an answer nor acknowledgment of receipt:

> In a *civilized* country one would be outraged by *the failure* of
> the head of Government even *to acknowledge receipt of a letter,*
> or to consider such a reasonable request put to him by a
> broadly representative collection of important personalities
> and leaders of the most important community of the country.
> Once again, Government standards in dealing with my people
> fell below what the *civilized* world would expect. No reply,
> no response whatsoever, was received to our letter, no indi-
> cation was even given that it had received any consideration
> whatsoever. Here we, the African people, and especially we
> of the National Action Council, who had been entrusted with
> the tremendous *responsibility* of safeguarding the interests of
> the African people, were faced with *this conflict between the
> law and our conscience.* (p. 145)

Not to acknowledge receipt is to betray the laws of civility
but first of all those of civilization: a primitive behavior, a
return to the state of nature, a presocial phase, *before the
establishment of the law.* Why does the Government return to
this noncivilized practice? Because it considers the majority

of the people, the "most numerous community," as noncivilized, before or outside the law. Acting in this way, interrupt-
ing the correspondence thus in a unilateral fashion, the white
man no longer respects his own law. He is blinded by this
evidence: a letter received means that the other is appealing
to the law of the community. In scorning his own law, the
white man gives the law over to being scorned:

> Perhaps the Court will say that despite our human rights to
> protest, to object, to make ourselves heard, we should stay
> within the letter of the law. I would say, Sir, that it is the
> Government, its administration of the law, which brings the
> law into such contempt and disrepute that one is no longer
> concerned in this country to stay within the letter of the law.
> I will illustrate this from my own experience. The Govern-
> ment has used the process of law to handicap me, in my
> personal life, in my career, and in my political work, in a
> way which is calculated, in my opinion, to bring about *con-
> tempt of the law.* (p. 148)

This scorn for the law (the symmetrical inverse of the *respect* for the moral law, as Kant would say: *Achtung/Verach-
tung)* is not then his, is not Mandela's. He reflects somehow,
by accusing, by answering, by acknowledging receipt, the
scorn of the whites for their own law. It is still and always a
reflection. Those who one day made him an outlaw just did
not have that right: they had already placed themselves outside
the law. By describing his own outlawed condition, Mandela
analyzes and reflects the outlawed being of the law in the
name of which he will have been not judged but persecuted,
prejudged, judged a criminal beforehand, as if, in this endless
trial, the trial had *already* taken place, before the investigation,
whereas it has been endlessly adjourned:

> I was made, by the law, a criminal, not because of what I
> had done, but because of what I stood for, because of what
> I thought, because of my conscience. Can it be any wonder
> to anybody that such conditions make a man an outlaw of

society? Can it be wondered that such a man, having been outlawed by the Government, should be prepared to lead the life of an outlaw, as I have led for some months, according to the evidence before this Court? ... But there comes a time, as it came in my life, when a man is denied the right to live a normal life, when he can only live the life of an outlaw because the Government has so decreed to use the law to impose a state of outlawry upon him. (pp. 148–149)

Mandela is thus accusing the white governments of never *answering* even as they demand that the blacks be quiet and use correspondence: resign yourself to correspondence and to corresponding all alone.

Sinister irony of a counterpoint: after his condemnation, Mandela is isolated twenty-three hours a day in a house in the center of Pretoria. He has to sew together postal bags.

4

A man of the law by vocation, Mandela submits the laws of his métier to the same reflection, professional deontology, its essence and its contradictions. This lawyer, enjoined by the "code of deontology to observe the laws of this country and to respect its traditions," how could he have conducted a campaign and incited others to strike against the politics of this same country? He asks this question himself in front of his judges. To answer it requires nothing less than the story of his life. The decision to conform or not to a code of deontology does not depend on deontology *as such*. The question "what to do about professional deontology, should one respect it or not?" is not of a professional order. It takes as a response a decision that engages one's whole existence in its moral, political, historical dimensions. In a way, one has to recount one's life in order to explain or rather to justify the transgression of a professional rule:

In order that the Court shall understand the frame of mind which leads me to action such as this, it is necessary for me

to explain the background to my own political development
and to try to make this Court aware of the factors which
influenced me in deciding to act as I did.

Many years ago, when I was a boy brought up in my village
in the Transkei . . . (p. 141)

Is Mandela treating professional obligations lightly? No, he
is trying to think through his profession, which is not just an
ordinary profession. He is reflecting the deontology of deontology, the deep meaning and the spirit of the deontological
laws. And once again by admiring respect, he decides to adopt
uncompromising measures in the name of a deontology of
deontology that is just as clearly a deontology beyond itself, a
law beyond legality. But the paradox of this reflection (the
deontology *of* deontology), which carries *beyond* what it reflects, is that responsibility takes on once again its meaning *in
the inside* of the professional apparatus. It is reinscribed therein,
for Mandela decides, to all appearances against the legal code,
to exercise his profession just where they wanted to keep him
from doing so. As a "lawyer worthy of that name," he sets
himself *against the code in the code,* reflects the code, but
making visible thereby just what the code in action rendered
unreadable. His reflection, once more, shows what phenomenality still kept in hiding. It does not re-produce, it produces the visible. This production of light is justice—moral
or political. For the phenomenal dissimulation must not be
confused with some natural process; it has nothing neutral
about it, either innocent or fatal. It translates here the political
violence of the whites, it holds to their interpretation of the
laws, to that proliferation of legal apparatuses and purviews
whose letter is destined to contradict the spirit of the law.
For example, because of the color of his skin and his belong-
ing to the Council for National Action, Mandela cannot oc-
cupy any professional premises in town. He must therefore,
unlike any white lawyer, have a special authorization from the
Government, conforming to the Urban Areas Act. Authorization refused. Then a waiver that is not renewed. Mandela

must from then on practice in an indigenous reservation, accessible only with difficulty to those who need his counsel in town:

> This was tantamount to asking us to abandon our legal practice, to give up the legal service of our people, for which we had spent many years training. No attorney worth his salt will agree easily to do so. For some years, therefore, we continued to occupy premises in the city, illegally. The threat of prosecution and ejection hung menacingly over us throughout that period. It was an act of *defiance of the law.* We were aware that it was, but, nevertheless, that act had been forced on us against our wishes, and we could do no other than to choose between compliance with the law and compliance with our consciences ... I regarded it as a duty which I owed, not just to my people, but also to my profession, to the practice of law, and to justice for all mankind, to cry out against this discrimination which is essentially unjust and opposed to the whole basis of the attitude towards justice which is part of the tradition of legal training in this country. (pp. 142–143)

A man of the law by vocation: it would be greatly simplifying things to say that he places respect for the law and a certain categorical imperative above professional deontology. The "profession of jurist" is not a métier like any other. It professes, we could say, what we are all bound to, even outside the profession. A jurist is an expert of respect or admiration, he judges or delivers himself to judgment with an increased rigor, or in any case he should. Mandela must then find, *inside* professional deontology, the best reason for failing in a legislative code which already betrayed the principles of every *good* professional deontology. As if, upon reflection, he were also to repair, supplement, reconstruct, add on to a deontology where the whites were finally showing themselves deficient.

Twice, then, he confesses a certain "scorn for the law" (still his expression) in order to hold out to his adversaries the mirror in which they should recognize and see their own contempt for the law being reflected. But with this *supplementary inversion:* on the side of Mandela, the apparent contempt signifies an increase of respect for the law.

However, he does not accuse his judges, not immediately, at least not in the moment when he appears before them. Doubtless he will first have objected to them: on one hand, the Court had as yet no black in its composition and thus offered no guarantees of the necessary impartiality ("The South African Government affirms that the Universal Declaration of the Rights of Man is applied in this country but, in truth, equality before the law in no way exists in relation to the concerns of our people"); on the other hand, the president happens to remain, between sessions, in contact with the political police. But once in front of his judges, these objections having of course not been sustained, Mandela no longer accuses the tribunal. First, he still maintains inside him this respectful admiration for those who exercise a function exemplary in his eyes and for the dignity of a tribunal. Then the respect of rules permits him to confirm the ideal legitimacy of an instance before which he also needs to *appear.* He wants to seize the occasion, I don't dare repeat the chance once more, of this trial in order to *speak,* to give to his word a space of *public* resonance, virtually universal. His judges must represent a universal instance. He will thus be able to speak to them, while speaking over their heads. This double opportunity permits him to gather together the meaning of his history, his and that of his people, in order to articulate it into a coherent account. The image of what allies his story to that of his people must form itself in this double focus, which at once welcomes it, gathers it up by drawing it together, and keeps it, yes, keeps it above all: the judges here present who are listening to Mandela, and behind them, rising high and far above them, the universal court. And in a while we find the man and the philosopher of this tribunal again. For once, then, there will have been a discourse aloud *and* correspondence, the written text of his pleading, which is also an indictment:

it has come over to us, here it is, we are reading it at this
very moment.

5

This text is at once unique and exemplary. Is it a *testament*?
What has become of it over the past twenty years? What has
history done, what will it do with it? What will become of the
example? And Nelson Mandela himself? His jailers dare speak
of exchanging him, negotiating for his freedom, bargaining for
his freedom and that of Sakharov.

There are two ways, at least, to receive a testament and
two senses of the word—two ways, in short, to acknowledge
receipt. One can inflect it toward what *bears witness* only to a
past and knows itself condemned to reflecting on what will
not return: a sort of West in general, the end of a trip which
is also the trajectory from a luminous source, the end of an
epoch, for example that of the Christian West (Mandela speaks
its language, he is also an English Christian). But, another in-
flection, if the testament is always made in front of witnesses,
a witness in front of witnesses, it is also to open and enjoin,
it is to confide in others the responsibility of a future. To bear
witness, to test, to attest, to contest, to present oneself before
witnesses. For Mandela, it was not only to show himself, to
give himself to be known, him and his people, it was also to
reinstitute the law for the future, as if, finally, it had never
taken place. As if, having never been respected, it were to
remain, this arch-ancient thing that had never been present,
as the future even—still now invisible.

These two inflections of the testament are not opposed:
they meet in the exemplarity of the example when it concerns
respect for the law. Respect for a person, Kant tells us, is first
addressed to the law of which this person only gives us the
example. Properly, respect is due only to the law, which is
its sole cause. And yet—it's the law—we must respect the
other for himself, in his irreplaceable singularity. It is true

that, as a person or a reasonable being, the other always bears witness, in his very singularity, to the respect for the law. He is exemplary in this sense. And still reflecting, according to the same optics, that of admiration and respect, these figures of the gaze. Some will be tempted to see in Mandela the witness or the martyr of the past. According to them, he let himself be captured (literally, imprisoned) in the view of the West, as in the machination of his reflecting apparatus; he has not only interiorized the law, we were saying, he has interiorized the principle of interiority in its testamentary tradition (Christian, Rousseauist, Kantian, and so on).

But one could say the opposite: his reflection lets us see, in the most singular geopolitical conjunction, in this extreme concentration of all human history that are the places or the stakes today called, for example, "South Africa," or "Israel," the promise of what has not yet ever been seen or heard, in a law that has not yet presented itself in the West, at the Western border, except briefly, before immediately disappearing. What will be decided in these so-called places—these are also formidable metonymies—would decide everything, if there were still that—everything.

So the exemplary witnesses are often those who distinguish between the law and laws, between respect for the law which speaks immediately to the conscience and submission to positive law (historical, national, institutional). Conscience is not only memory but promise. The exemplary witnesses, those who make us think about the law they reflect, are those who, in certain situations, *do not respect* laws. They are sometimes torn between conscience and law, they are sometimes condemned by the tribunals of their country. And there are some in *every country*, which proves that the place where these things occur is also for the law the place of the first uprooting. For example, in England a peer of the Realm (still this admiration for the most elevated forms of parliamentary democracy), a philosopher who is the "most respected in the Western world," knew how, in certain situations, not to respect the law, how to put "conscience," "duty," "faith in the justice of the cause" before the "respect for the law." It is out of respect that he did not show respect: no more respect. Respect for the sake of respect. Can we regulate some optical model on what such a possibility promises?

Admiration of Mandela—for Bertrand Russell:

> Your Worship, I would say that the whole life of any thinking African in this country drives him continuously to a conflict between his conscience on the one hand and the law on the other. This is not a conflict peculiar to this country. The conflict arises for men of conscience, for men who think and who feel deeply in every country. Recently in Britain, a peer of the realm, Earl Russell, probably *the most respected* philosopher of the Western world, was sentenced, convicted for precisely the type of activities for which I stand before you today, for following his conscience in defiance of the law, as a protest against a nuclear-weapons policy being followed by his own government. For him, his duty to the public, his belief in the morality of the essential rightness of the cause for which he stood, rose superior to his *high respect for the law.* He could not do other than to oppose the law and to suffer the consequences for it. Nor can I. Nor can many Africans in this country. The law as it is applied, the law as it has been developed over a long period of history, and especially the law as it is written and designed by the Nationalist Government, is a law which, in our view, is immoral, unjust, and intolerable. Our consciences dictate that we must protest against it, that we must oppose it, and that we must attempt to alter it. (pp. 143–144)

To oppose the law, to then try and transform it: once the decision is made, the recourse to violence should not take place without measure and without rule. Mandela explains in minute detail the strategy, the limits, the progress reflected upon and observed. First there was a phase in the course of which, all legal opposition being forbidden, the infraction had nevertheless to remain nonviolent:

All lawful modes of expressing opposition to this principle had been closed by legislation, and we were placed in a position in which we had either to accept a permanent state of inferiority or to defy the Government. We chose to defy the law. We first broke the law in a way which avoided any recourse to violence. (p. 156)

The infraction still manifests the absolute respect of the supposed spirit of the law. But it was impossible to stop there. For the Government invented new legal devices to repress nonviolent challenges. To this violent response, which was also a nonresponse, the passage to violence was in its turn the only possible response. Response to the nonresponse:

When this form was legislated against, and then the Government resorted to a show of force to crush opposition to its policies, only then did we decide to answer violence with violence. (Ibid)

But there again, the violence remains subject to a rigorous law, "a strictly controlled violence." Mandela insists, he underlines these words at the moment when he explains the genesis of the *Umkonto we Sizwe* (the Nation's Spear) in November 1961. In founding that combative organization, he means to submit it to the political directives of the Council for National Action, whose statutes prescribe nonviolence. In front of his judges, Mandela describes in detail the rules of action, the strategy, the tactics, and above all the limits imposed on the militants charged with sabotage: to wound or kill no one, either in the preparation or the execution of the operations. The militants must not bear arms. If he recognizes "having prepared a plan of sabotage," it was neither through "adventurism" nor through any "love of violence in itself." On the contrary, he wanted to interrupt what is so oddly called the cycle of violence, one implying the other because first of all it answers, reflects, sends it back its image. Mandela meant to limit the risks of explosion in controlling the actions of the militants, in constantly devoting himself to what he calls a "reflective" analysis of the situation.

He is arrested four months after the creation of the *Umkonto,* in August 1962. In May 1964, at the end of the trial of Rivonia, he is condemned to permanent criminal detention.

P.S. The postscript is for the future—for that part of the future most undecided today. I wanted to speak, of course, of Nelson Mandela's future, of what does not allow itself to be anticipated, caught, captured by any mirror. Who is Nelson Mandela?

We will never cease to admire him, himself and his admiration. But we don't yet know whom to admire in him, the one who, in the past, will have been the captive of his admiration or the one who, in a future anterior, will always have been free (the freest man in the world, let us not say that lightly) for having had the patience of his admiration and having known, passionately, what he had to admire. The one refusing as early as yesterday a conditioned freedom.

Would they have also imprisoned him, almost a quarter of a century ago, in his admiration itself? Was that not the *objective*—I mean that in the sense of photography and of the optic machine—the right to look? Did he *let* himself be imprisoned? Did he *have* himself imprisoned? Was that an accident? Perhaps we should place ourselves at a point where these alternatives lose their meaning and become the justification and the starting point for new questions. Then leave these questions still open, like doors. And what remains to be seen in these questions, which are not only theoretical or philosophical, is also the figure of Mandela. Who is he?

We have looked at him through words which are sometimes the devices for observation, which can in any case become that if we are not careful. What we have described, in trying precisely to escape speculation, was a sort of great historical watchtower or observation post. But nothing permits us to imagine this unity as assured, still less the legitimacy of this optic of reflection, of its singular laws, of the law, of its place of institution, of presentation or of revelation, for example of what we assemble too quickly under the name of the West. But doesn't this presumption of unity produce something like an effect (I don't hold to this word) that so many forces, always, try to appropriate for themselves? An effect visible and invisible, like a mirror, also hard, like the walls of a prison.

All that still hides Nelson Mandela from our sight.

Translated from the French by Mary Ann Caws and Isabelle Lorenz

SAMUEL
BECKETT

▼

BRIEF DREAM

Go end there
One fine day
Where never till then
Till as much as to say
No matter where
No matter when

SUSAN SONTAG

THIS MAN, THIS COUNTRY

▼

A political prisoner is in jail, under sentence of life imprisonment, since 1964; but many men and women on this planet are imprisoned, detained, silenced for their political views and activities. The majority of the inhabitants of a country are disenfranchised and oppressed; but majorities in many countries around the world are deprived of democratic liberties and social justice.

Why *this* man? Why *this* country?

This man is exemplary. Because of who he is, how he has behaved, what he has said (and goes on saying); because the cause of which he has been for decades a preeminent leader is just; and because his version of it is the most mature, politically and morally, the most realistic, the one most likely to lead to reconciliation and to avoid the otherwise inevitable carnage. Outside his prison, he has a wife, daughters, friends, comrades, who, operating under dire constraints, unremitting harassment, and great danger, continue his struggle. He would like to be free. But he will not accept anything less than an unconditional liberty. He has refused, more than once, a conditional release. He has said that he will not negotiate with his captors, since a prisoner, someone who is not free, cannot enter into contracts. This of course is not, strictly speaking, true. One *can* negotiate in captivity for one's freedom—if it is one's own freedom only. But he understands that his freedom is not just his own, that it is (if he so chooses) linked indissolubly to the freedom of the people he represents. He cannot negotiate *their* freedom as a captive.

It is often said that this man is a "symbol." But no one is inherently a symbol. Someone becomes a symbol, is made a symbol, as this man has been. The few moral heroes—and this man *is* a moral hero—who become celebrated (as distinct from the many heroes who do not) do so under the pressure of historical need. The practice of singling out as exemplary one person—specifically, one prisoner or victim—illustrates the way in which all affections and attachments inevitably must become institutionalized, acquire titles, engender hierarchies, in order to have historical weight: to be political. Inevitable, too, in this process are some corruptions of feeling and distortions of truth and of response. Still, when the struggle is just and the behavior of the prisoner really exemplary, such singling out is not only ineluctable but positive. It is right that this man has been made a symbol.

He represents not only aspirations held by most people around the world but a very large community in his own country, who acknowledge him as their leader. He is in opposition, he is in prison. But he is not a "dissident." That is why he cannot be treated as a common political prisoner, hidden away, starved, beaten, humiliated, cut off from contacts with relatives and with the outside world. This man, in prison, receives (or refuses to receive) important visitors to his country, like the major political figure that he is. Tacit head of a political party which, although it plays no formal political role and has its headquarters in exile, already wields major power; de facto head-of-state, the president of a democratic country that does not yet exist but will exist, he is both a symbol, living in what is (given the present realities of his country) an aptly symbolic place, a prison, and a very real political force.

Of course, it is the present undemocratic racist government that permits him this role—as the British, even when they imprisoned Gandhi, were obliged to detain him under conditions that reflected his immense political power and moral influence, the power (that is, the mounting ungovern-ability) of the vast community outside the prison which he continued to represent. But it was not always so for him. The early years of his imprisonment, on Robben Island, were as harsh as any Gulag; and there was no communication with the outside, no parleying with foreign dignitaries who could report being "first struck . . . by his immaculate appearance, his apparent good health, and his commanding presence. In his manner he exuded authority and received the respect of all around him, including his gaolers." (I quote from the re-port issued in 1986 by "The Commonwealth Eminent Persons Group on Southern Africa.") Only in the last years, since the community he represents has had to be reckoned with by the present government, has he been granted this status. The gov-ernment would like nothing more than to strike a "deal," and to release him. But he refuses a conditional release because he is in a position of strength.

Becoming the subject of an international campaign for his release does not confer this status on a prisoner; political realities, both domestic and international, do that. Andrei Sak-harov was at least as famous and morally admired a political prisoner as this man, but the fact is that Sakharov represents mostly his own exemplary courage and the rightness of his views. The government that detained him until recently knew that he represented no threat; the deal to be struck was with world public opinion, not with its own citizenry.

We called for liberty for Sakharov, for Irina Ratushinskaya, and for the many more imprisoned unjustly in that country (among others) because we wanted these precious people to survive: what we were asking for was clemency. For Sakharov, Ratushinskaya, and others, there was no difference between a conditional and an unconditional release. They wanted, we wanted for them, to get out.

With this man, it is different. We do not simply seek his liberty; we respect his decision to remain in prison. We be-lieve the days of this government are numbered. To release this prisoner is to bring the fall of the apartheid government much closer. We seek his freedom not just on the grounds of compassion but on political grounds. For his liberty, when he has it, will be a major step toward the liberation of the majority of his compatriots.

He is not free inside prison now, but he is powerful. He is powerful because of the trust that flows to him from the community he represents. We seek his freedom because we seek the freedom of the majority of the inhabitants of his country. His freedom is theirs. He has made it so. (He could have lived his imprisonment otherwise.) We demand his freedom. And the freedom of those for whom he is imprisoned.

This man. This country.

ALLEN GINSBERG

FAR AWAY

▼▼

They say Blacks work sweating
in hot mines thousands of feet
deep in mountains of South Africa
to bring up gold & diamonds shining
on earth into the hands of White
bankers, politicians, police & armies.

"ON THE CONDUCT OF THE WORLD
SEEKING BEAUTY AGAINST GOVERNMENT"

▽

Is that the only way we can become like Indians, like
         Rhinoceri,
like Quartz Crystals, like organic farmers, live what we
         imagine
Adam & Eve to've been, caressing each other with trembling
         limbs
before the Snake of Revolutionary Sex wrapped itself round
The Tree of Knowledge? What would Roque Dalton joke about
         lately
teeth chattering like a machine gun as he debated mass
         tactics
with his Compañeros? Necessary to kill the Yanquis with a
         big bomb
Yes but don't do it by yourself, better consult your mother
to get the Correct Line of Thought, if not consult Rimbaud
         once he got his leg cut off
or Lenin after his second stroke sending a message thru
         Mrs. Krupskaya
to the rude Georgian, & just before his deathly fit when
         the Cheka aides outside
his door looked in coldly assuring him his affairs were
         in good hands
no need to move—What sickness at the pit of his stomach
         moved up to his brain?

What thought Khlebnikov on the hungry train exposing his
        stomach to the sun?
Or Mayakovsky before the bullet hit his brain, what sharp
        propaganda for Action
on the Bureaucratic Battlefield in the Ministry of Collective
        Agriculture in Ukraine?
What Slogan for Futurist architects or epic hymn for masses
        of Communist Party Card holders in Futurity
on the conduct of the world seeking beauty against Government?

JORGE
AMADO

NELSON MANDELA
IN BRAZIL

▼

We Brazilians have known Nelson Mandela quite well, not just today, but for a long time. We know his deepest intimacy, the silence imposed on him, and his poetry as it spreads more and more freely throughout the world. If the truth be known, we have had him here alive among us for four centuries. It's not hard to find him on the streets of any Brazilian city, large or small, it's easy to recognize him in the face of a dark-skinned child with cat eyes and tight curly hair. Finding it a nice and important-sounding name, in holy innocence his father hung that of an English Lord of the Admiralty on him, but his family name has the savor of an ancient and proud African nation: *malë, mandinda, mandela.* He's poor—almost all of our people are very poor—but his laughter is quick and vibrant. He's free to run on the beach and in the hills, to play with his blood brothers with differing skin tones, all from the same mixture of black, Indian, and European blood, to undertake his own particular adventure in life in the big world. From that noteworthy human condition, it is he who demands, from Brazilian soil on the other side of the Atlantic, with just and deep-seated reasons, unconditional freedom for the African poet, his ancestor and his brother.

He can be found around here, everywhere, at every moment. Less than a month ago a group of us, a few intellectuals from Brazil and several African countries, were visiting the Serra da Barriga (Belly Hills) in the northeastern Brazilian state of Alagoas. Some of the visitors were educated young Senegalese, the heirs to *Négritude,* the movement started by Léopold Sendar Senghor that holds the country today and whose basic thrust is for autonomous cultural development to be the basis of all social progress, a lesson that makes them anxious to build their own civilization in a free country through contacts with people who are their brothers. They wanted to touch the ground of the Serra da Barriga with their own hands, and when they got there they stood in awed silence. The African had come to Brazil in chains in the hold of a slaver and he remained a slave for four centuries. The history of slavery in Brazil, however, is that of a continuous struggle against oppression, against the terror imposed by the white colonist. The amazing part of that struggle is the fact that two centuries before the abolition of slavery in the nation, right there in the seventeenth century, blacks organized a flight from slave quarters, plantations, and cities and, in the forests of Alagoas, they founded the Republic of Palmares, the first black republic anywhere in the world. They maintained and consolidated an island of freedom in a sea of slavery for many decades. The young African intellectuals stood in silence when they got there, mute and humble, as in the nave of a church. Palmares today is a national monument, preserved by law for all the people. The day we were there, a Brazilian poet demanded freedom for Nelson Mandela and his people. With perfectly logical poetic license, he coupled the name of the imprisoned African poet to that of Zumbi of Palmares, the leader of the black republic, declaring that the struggle of both of them, separated by three centuries and an ocean, was the same and with the same almost insurmountable conditions, with the same certainty of hope and victory.

I came across Mandela again last week at the auditorium of the university at a meeting of students of Spanish language and literature. The theme was the hatred dictatorships bear toward poets and poetry. I reminded the young people of my country that precisely a half-century ago the dictator Franco's assassins roused up the Andalusian Gypsy, Federico García

Lorca, in the middle of the night and in the middle of his short life and, in the name of that blind hatred, shot him. A student recited the stark condemnation of Antonio Machado's verses: "The crime took place in Granada, his Granada!" We recalled together, the young students and I, the loving poetry, cool as a mountain breeze, of Miguel Hernández, the gentle goatherd who had appeared one day in Madrid when the first bombs of the war were falling, and linked his startlingly revealing poetry to that of Rafael Alberti, Jorge Guillén, Antonio and Manuel Machado, and so many others, to form one of the highest poetical moments of all times. Miguel Hernández was murdered slowly in a filthy Spanish prison. A young black girl arose then and brought up the theme of the hatred of dictatorships for poets in the here and now as she started to read a poem by Nelson Mandela. The meeting ended with the drawing up of the short text of a telegram to be sent to the South African Ambassador to Brazil, brief and revealing, like a line of poetry: "You people are afraid of Nelson Mandela!"

Translated from the Portuguese by Gregory Rabassa

JOHN
ASHBERY

DRAB SHUTTERS

The whole family is keenly interested in money.
Of course, there are ways out, ways
You never thought of
Before, so interested in the sun
And everything it shines on
You want to explore, explore's the word
For all that happens to us, rains down on us,
Makes us come apart
In the middle of some perfectly okay conversation
About what the prehistoric monsters did, what routes they took
Out of the chasm of their being unable to survive,
Of how extinction thoughtfully embraced each one,
Even the startling pterodactyl,
And sealed its fate with a kiss.

But today, you see, is different.
The rent in the sky has been mended
That annoyed people on earth so long
Its invisibility became a chore,
And we are sealed up
In our climatized jungle habitat, that's so vast
That variations on it are unlikely
For at least a century, but
You can put down that book.
And walk out into the world
The illustration has become.

And it's back to instances,
To proceeding case by case to the one
Irreducible situation the zippered sky had outlawed,
Though it's almost too old now: young, but still past its prime.
When he threw her at the dishes
And the Darjeeling splashed
It tasted warm, was stamped "good" so as to
Shovel all this under the figured rug.
There must be no exclamation point; italics, too,
Are suspect, and I
Don't know how I got down here, but know
I must thank someone for it, otherwise the game, the day will
    be lost
And the gray return again, to seize us like tweed.
In case you thought we had an emergency here.

Well, it's true. I rub my eyes
As much as anybody and don't know how the world (read:
    "my world")
Is going to survive *this* one, yet again,
That killed vaudeville once, all up and down the east coast
As far west as Ashtabula. I always forget
How you can't see in the dark, but I see
That tribes have gathered in this last, plush valley
Under a millennial tree, to sort out, bathe
And remove the last vestiges of ambiguous
Truth, of European civilization, and our arrival
May be shuttered in dark early morning, better
Than the time it took to get here
And all the wonderful things we came to see.

MICHEL
LEIRIS

APARTHEID

▼

Apartheid: I know neither the exact pronunciation of this word nor its etymology. But I do know that when I read it I always think of the adjective "hideous" because of its resemblance with the final syllable. As for its initial vowel, I take it to be a privative prefix as befits this designation of a cruel and absurd policy since it is one that aims to bar certain people from partaking fully and completely in the human species, of which all of us, regardless of our color, are representatives. *Apartheid:* a harsh, mean word that resounds in one's ears like a trapdoor opening beneath a gallows.

Translated from the French by Peggy Kamuf

MUSTAPHA
TLILI

THE FUTURE ITSELF

▼▼

The story of Horia, an old woman living alone on the Tunisian steppe, is from a novel in progress entitled (provisionally?) A Thousand Futures Lost, and concerns an adamant struggle to keep a beloved horizon pure, and to keep sovereign a freedom felt as a native, inalienable good.

The frail, weak Horia, with the inflexibility of a powerful inner vision, unshakably resists large forces. These forces rise up against the old woman and build constructions justified only by tricky schemes, but which deprive Horia of the open and unobstructed view, which she has always had from her ancestral home, of the ocher mountain proudly standing in the distance. A Thousand Futures Lost will be about resisting the intolerable.

The extract appearing here, voiced by a narrator anguished with regrets—should he not have come to Horia's aid when there was still time?—is a draft of the old woman's happiness before injustice strikes. It is dedicated to the proud and indomitable Winnie Mandela— who is not old and who is not alone and who is the future itself.

The day had to come when I would say good-bye to this beloved land. With every emotion checked, every pain unexpressed, every sob held back, I must accept my turn to die.

To detach myself, with no hope or desire of returning to this dawn, to its sweet fragile air, to its horizon vibrant with pale blue light tinged with delicate pinks.

I must accept tearing myself for good from the blessed sight of the sovereign ocher mountain there, Lion Mountain, blood-red on a summer evening when the passionate, already African sun of the Tunisian steppe sets it ablaze in moments of supreme glory, then swallows it up with the entire sky and its streaming golds.

The words will come unhurriedly. Regrets and pain will not divert them from their course, which I want to be serene. Strangely, not even a week after the drama, I already sense all is calm in me. But wouldn't Horia have wanted it that way, for me to brave man's hour of final reckoning, to be calm when the moment for the last turning of the page has indeed come?

The cool dawn wearing its fine, nearly diaphanous veil of crimson . . . The glowing dusk settling on Lion Mountain leaves a thousand waves of purple on its slopes and along the whole horizon. Dawn and dusk are rent by the muezzin's chant calling the faithful to prayer here in this tiny village lost in the vast Tunisian steppe. When I attempt in a single movement to grasp Horia's memory, the images are clear and simple. They come back powerful, haunting, like the rhythm of her life since we her children left for the city and the world, marked by those strong double beats of the cosmos and God, dawn and dusk. I remember, it was like this especially in summer when I would return from America for a few eagerly anticipated days of vacation and happiness in her company.

Early in the morning Horia is already on site in front of our place, a wide, low Moorish house ornamented with mara-bout domes and softly white with the coarse lime applied at the start of each summer. The old woman performs her ablutions in the brook peacefully flowing past the house, a familiar melody in the vast surrounding wilderness. She is readying herself for prayers, all collectedness and piety, but filled with a singular, almost pagan sense of contentment. And at this hour, favored by the lions of an earlier age, in the vast stony semiarid stretch that rises seamlessly, with a few low hills here and there, from our house to the ocher mountain looming majestically in the distance, rarely a soul goes by.

Again, late in the afternoon, with the steppe's grueling blaze banked, subdued, and receptive to the soon-triumphant reign of miraculous twilight, harbinger of delightful coolness and matchless well-being, here is Horia outside in front of her house. Humbly, she prepares to yield every fiber of her being to the will of God, but she still feels exalted by the singular sensation she had at dawn.

Both morning and evening, at dawn as at dusk, her duty toward God accomplished, Horia sits down on her prayer rug and in complete abandon leans back to the cool wall of her low white house. As though absent, lulled by the brook's thin crystalline music telling her and the steppe the epic of the lords of the ocher mountain, life and passing time, she is engaged in intense meditation, a long contemplation of the finely drawn line of the horizon before her, which she sees without any obstacle to separate it from where she sits, from in front of her home, her realm in this world. She looks, never tiring, at this marvel offered for the delectation of a lonely old woman who no longer expects big things in life. She admires this pure and perfect line, all plenitude that cannot suffer the least interference, the horizon of the ocher mountain, the mountain of the lion. And what the old woman admires is assuredly pride itself, eternity, even if to Horia's heart and mind eternity can have but one unique name—God.

Forgotten is the steppe in winter with its rigors, its long black frigid nights. The miracle is here. The breeze, the breeze. The coolness once again desired.

The soul shrinks no more. Horia's being no longer invents another life for itself. It no longer takes refuge in the bright hot colors of the *kilims* she weaves for us, or for us to give our friends in Tunis, Paris, or New York. Compositions in wool that she has washed, carded, spun, dyed—her labor from start to finish. Abstract designs that she creates, winter after winter, to be given away. A thousand geometries in luxuriant tints, of abundant love and brimming hope that save one from oneself and from solitude and hurl an ultimate defiance at death.

Winter is behind her, and also the effort required of the frail

Horia for the symmetries of these figures fitted together in seam-
less delicacy and multiplied in charming variations. Naively
splendid, but deeply imbued with exacting necessity. She creates
this composition of beauty with no other plan than that prescribed—from moment to moment of absolute concentration
and fascination—by the deflection inspired by a particular blood
red, the translation spontaneously suggested by a midnight blue,
the thematic representation born in the wake of an insistent
black, the resumption in parallel or closure dictated by this brilliant white. And how can this extravagant adventure in colors
and shapes, correspondences and harmony, which obeys such
imperious inherent constraints, not become the only destiny that
matters to Horia in the days and nights on the hard winter steppe?
How can she not invest herself completely in this captivating
song—absent to the rest, absent to the world?

But in the triumphal hours of summer dawn and dusk, in the
delicious moments of supreme communion and powerful happiness, the winter is no more. Now, Horia's expansive, conquer-
ing soul does not flee to some paradise of art. No, it is the
universe itself and its glory that claim Horia, taking hold of her
and swelling her and carrying her to the meeting of heaven and
earth, from Lion Mountain and the thousand other mountains
veiled in light blue or pale rose, beyond the songs that come
from afar. Voices resounding through time, the folds and re-
cesses of the mountain range and the steppe, which merge all,
without end. Their murmurs are taken up in sweet melody by
the little brook flowing at Horia's feet, in the silence and peace
of dawn or dusk, and, in the light coolness of supreme rapture,
they tell of her ancestors and their epic, begun in lost Andalusia.

For all the land, this dwelling place, the ocher mountain over
there, the pure, ecstatically beautiful line of the horizon, the
serene expanse surrounding Horia have always been the sacred
undivided property of her and of hers, going back, as far as she
can trace, to the time of her ancestors and in some other time
of uncertain origins.

From earliest childhood Horia has lived on the legend of the
scholar-warrior lords who fled Andalusia, which the infidels had

won back from them after they refused to give up their faith and renounce the rank which they owed to their knowledge and commerce with the mind—a vision whose authenticity, she assures us, is forever attested to by the very existence of Lion Mountain across from the little brook.

Horia sees and hears again the ride of the knights of the steppe, the tribal banner proudly displayed at their head flapping in the hot dusty winds of the vast reaches of North Africa.

All through dawn and dusk, the ancestors go racing by, looming up from the other side of the ocher mountain. This land is theirs, their haven, their place of redemption. They claim it, and it claims them, they possess it for all time.

In Horia's head the thunder of the cavalcade grows louder. The lords of the mountain, victors over all adversities, a thousand wars, a thousand defeats, a thousand triumphs forgotten behind them, their blood and their flesh, their spirit and their lights strewn from Gibraltar to here, this far with the slow passage of years, centuries, there they are, proclaimed by the soon-deafening resonance of the final charge of the immense exhausted cavalcade. They appear at the glowing horizon, draw near, and rush down the side of the ocher mountain, Lion Mountain, desired by this land that wants them, calls to them, and to which they call.

Land of one's ancestors, the ancestors from this ocher land—arid, poor, but loved, yes, loved by Horia, the land of that venerated mountain.

Origin of time passing, and of this brook flowing in the peace of the steppe, at dawn, at dusk.

Origin of this home that Horia leans on—slight, stooped, and gnarled body, like an ancient stunted oleander in a long-dry riverbed whipped by the searing wind.

The echo of the cavalcade becomes unbearable in Horia's head, bound winter and summer in scarves for fear of the cold and its ills. Always the same image, always the same inherited vision of the legend of the steppe, faithfully passed on by her insouciant brook.

▲ ▲

Or at night. These too-hot summer nights are stifling in the white rooms, in the patio, near the patches of mint and jars full of water that no breeze comes to cool, giving lie to the urban myth that summer nights on the steppe are chilly.

Horia is outside, leaning on her house, as solid as she, like the weight of centuries. In the absolute darkness where no light appears, she is engrossed in contemplation of the sky bending under its millions of stars. She is enchanted by this black roof brimming with gold above her.

Horia cannot read and write. No matter, the starry universe and its majesty, presented for her admiration, are the answer to all questions in those moments of deep meditation and when she is bathed in the silence of the night and caressed by the light breeze from the mountain, filled with thyme, rosemary, and other delightful scents.

A powerful feeling comes over her—there is infinity, beautiful and awesomely organized. Down the centuries and on for eternity, we and our ambitions, triumphs and defeats, joys and sorrows, are merely an element in a harmonious whole that a supreme being wills to be so. The starry sky above is peopled with angels, prophets, God's messengers, the voices of the good perpetually reminding us of our destiny. Written by our Creator, the text of the universe is readable and clear in itself—he who sincerely desires the truth has no need for other learning. Who, intimately, does not know his duty? she asks me. Who, in the bottom of his heart, does not see evil?

Horia grew up as a daughter of the steppe. The elders were careful to preserve any future wife from the world's temptations, from reading and writing—paths of men, ways of the best and also the worst. With all her energies, she devoted herself to pushing us, her children, toward learning. To be worthy heirs of the lords of the ocher mountain. And because, for Horia, knowledge, the domain of men, is not just learning, civility, manners, but also, more than all else, a means of access to the sacred, and thereby a chance for the soul's salvation.

▲ ▲

She never stops reminding us that this land, this dwelling, this black and silent expanse have been blessed ever since the scholar-warrior lords of the ocher mountain ended their exile, sweeping back from their lost kingdom, lured by the solitude of the places and by the miraculous coolness of a spring gushing forth in the secrecy of Lion Mountain. The trace is there for us—her children, their children—to follow. When one is descended from ancestors like these, when one is the son of a land like this, what possible destiny is there than to keep this imperious tradition alive?

To read, to write, to go toward the world and its cities, Tunis, Paris, New York . . . Horia weaves the *kilims* in the harsh winter nights. We give them away as presents. We will not forget, however. How can that be, never forget? We will tell our friends in Tunis, Paris, and New York that we are from this land. We are its proud sons.

We will bring our friends with us, the friends from New York or Paris.

We will even bring our "Western women with golden fleeces," tall and slim—to Horia so marvelously lean, so different from the women of this land. We, too, will come with them, since such is the outcome of our sacred quest for knowledge. Horia will praise them and receive them in the warmth of her heart.

But let us always claim kinship with this land, she would entreat us, for it is blessed by the lords of the ocher mountain and we are their worthy sons, and what matter if Horia cannot read and write.

Translated from the French by Franklin Philip

JUAN
GOYTISOLO

IN THE ICY WATERS
OF SELFISH CALCULATION

▼

It seems that Third Worldism, ill named from the start, has gone completely out of style. In today's Europe, lazily entangled in its moral mediocrity and military and economic dependence, a mere reminder of existing iniquities between North and South, rich countries and poor countries, now prompts a shrugging of shoulders, if not faces of outright disgust. I don't want to hear at this point about your Third World!

Can it be that that reality—far too distant and hazy, faded and trivialized on TV—has deserted the horizon of our lives? Its presence in Europe's communal pastures of created interests is nonetheless too obvious for us to dismiss it with a wave of the hand: twelve million immigrants, according to the statistics which, by extracting the significant part of the document from the void of the white page—I cite Genet from memory—are an annoying reminder of something unpleasant unless, like a chameleon, one blends by mere reflected movement into desired invisibility. The Eurocrat, new or old, doesn't want to see them. Happily he dubs himself a *hodgepodge,* selfish, noncommittal, hedonistic, Reaganistic. Happily, so that things appear well adjusted, without *complexes.* Ex-communists, Maoists, Guevarists, and de-Leninized socialists have changed their course, like a school of little red fish, to warmer, more serene waters. They say, like the ineffable Marguerite

Duras, that the present occupant of the White House embodies *the values of our times.* The harsh, Orwellian truth of the Soviet system, prevailing misery and tyranny in the Afro-Asiatic countries and Latin America justify the consumption of that dialectic pap, the self-satisfaction of those who have already turned back, and those who have never even left: rubbed out with a stroke of the pen are exploitation, poverty, racism, covert aggression, and overt aggression. Let us love our world with its imperfections. Let us love, above all, ourselves.

Living in the large European cities, we have little by little gotten used to the hygienic pawn, social and moral, of rubbing out writing that reveals our sickly pallor and substituting the black ink with another, invisible and secret kind, or one only legible if held up against the light: a chimerical transparency imposed on Arabs and West Indians, Central and West Africans, Pakistanis and Turks. With it comes a new punishable crime, the disobedience of looking like *a shady character:* different pigmentation of the skin, color and texture of the hair, arrogance in the style of mustache or way of dress, in short, *a shady-looking character.* They will attract like a magnet hostile looks from police, guards, wardens, watchmen, the upper and lower bourgeoisie, and the blue-collar worker, crazed by the phantom of unemployment. Those guilty of looking *shady* will carefully be separated from other riders on subway platforms and passages, pointed out, or rather *sifted* out of parks and streets, forced to identify themselves and show proof to disprove their external signs of alienation, subjected to thorough friskings, pushed into paddy wagons with sirens and roving lights, and regaled with the standard delicacies of a cozy police station. Over and over, the same numbing spectacle: *shadiness* resists shock therapy; it is, as we all know, difficult to eradicate.

The apocalyptic predictions made by the pale or rosy faces with porcine eyes and flabby double chins regarding the social danger that to them a foreign and insolent beauty embodies—

formulated on TV by *national* leaders, and circulated in turn
by tabloid journalism—trigger the protective reflexes of the
beleaguered good citizen. A brief review of the list of pre-
ventative measures of self-protection culled by the French
press constitutes an eloquent array of extremely ingenious ini-
tiatives: two Senegalese burned alive in their house by three
legionnaires, a North African hurled from a train going over
eighty miles an hour, three Turks gunned down in a café by
a hotheaded follower of Carlos Martel and Vercingétorix. Effective corrective measures, blows against the perverse crime
of looking *shady.*

But that's just the tip of the iceberg. Who really knows,
apart from those involved, the xenophobia, exploitation, and
scorn suffered day after day? One would have to dress, assume
the color and external traits of a foreigner as Gunter Wallraff
did for two years in order to penetrate the real world of *a
shady-looking character.* His book, *Head of a Turk,* is compelling
not because it introduces us to an exotic world—the Turkish
community living in Germany—but because it mercilessly ex-
poses our own X ray. That the author encounters in the middle of West Germany situations faithfully described in the
novels of Dickens and Zola is no real surprise; any observer
without blinders on can confirm it *de visu.* What gives special
value to the book—to its admirable telling of the adventure of
a solitary swimmer *in the icy waters of selfish calculation*—is the
author's "new look, richer and more extensive" at his compatriots' "poverty of spirit and icy indifference." There, yes,
there we hit on something, and Wallraff's vision, endowed
with a gift similar to that of King Midas, exoticizes whatever
he touches: decked out in his flashy new Turkish look, he
confines both himself and us to regulation hell with a sanctity
colored with humor and irony, and with an indignation that
pours out in a burst of uncontrollable laughter. The marginal
quality of his point of view sets it apart, and seems to cast an
aura of exceptional novelty over everyday, banal situations,
turning his world around, and converting it into a ridiculous

backdrop. It takes on symbolic meaning when Frau Willi, the funeral director, is ready to agree to a 10 percent discount on the price of the future repatriation of the corpse of a Turkish worker who is dying of cancer—if all expenses are guaranteed in advance. How can we not recognize in her the monstrosity of our friendly and obliging neighbor?

The almost picaresque job rounds made by the undercover Ali are those of twelve million Asian, Black, Arab, or Latin American *shady-looking characters,* who are constantly confronted by circumstances in which this monstrous behavioral norm leisurely unfolds. Wallraff, explorer of the limits of human degradation, compels us to probe unsuspected depths and go down laughing into the nauseating intestines of superior, refined, and civilized Europe. With quiet heroism he will accept the role, pariah among pariahs, of guinea pig for the flourishing pharmaceutical industry to discover that "behind the pleasant, smiling front of a cosmetic merchant lies a cool, modern Dr. Mabuse who offers chemical experimentation to those who have fallen into poverty, with a purely commercial strategy toward maximum interests of big business." But his experience of day-to-day horror doesn't stop there. In the nuclear energy plants of West Germany, denounces Wallraff, they recommend hiring temporary immigrant workers, ignorant of the risk they run, to clean and repair the equipment and contaminated areas of the plant. For a 500-mark reward, Ali or Mehmet will pack in in a few hours, maybe minutes, 5,000 *rems,* the maximum annual dose of radiation. In the event of an accident or leak, a common occurrence, envoys to the *red alert* zone will almost always be selected because of their *shadiness.* The cost of the operation is less, and accountability vague and impossible to prove. Who could accuse, years after the fact, Europe's immaculate centers of nuclear energy of the proliferation of cancer and leukemia in Maghreb or Anatolia?

If the scanty information on the dangers of nuclear energy leads the average citizen to accept with almost cheery fatalism the likelihood of a catastrophe in exchange for a good job, the illiteracy and innocence of immigrants turn them into perfect subjects for all kinds of experimentation and dirty work. This is not only true in Germany, where Wallraff documents the evidence, but in other European countries: in a recent radioactive leak in France, those exposed were "temporary workers contracted from a firm specializing in difficult and potentially risky jobs," a euphemism, no doubt, to avoid the word "foreigners." Turks in Germany, Arabs in France, Pakistanis in the United Kingdom, the most docile candidates for radioactive exposure will in any case purge their sin of looking *shady*. Only the Soviet Union, because of the government's absolute lack of information, can permit itself the luxury, as in Chernobyl, of treating its own citizens like foreign subjects, push them toward sure death, and then decorate them with the posthumous title of "socialist heroes." (In Spain we run a similar risk, unless the nuclear energy centers had the foresight to hire a percentage of gypsies.)

Exploring the depths of infamy that his countrymen could reach, Wallraff forces us to ask ourselves the question: How many thousand *rems* of villainy can a man of normal appearance accept without losing face or his smile? The case of Adler, a man well aware that he was leading his team of Turkish workers to their death, is absolutely electrifying, and in itself makes the book worth reading. Wallraff measures the level of moral radiation that a dignified conman like Adler is capable of, and the figures are astronomical: the meter's needle jumps at the impact of each new *shady* Turk, and the dizzying rate at which it rises never seems to stop. Thanks to Wallraff, we can know the thousands of *rems* of infamy absorbed by *Homo sapiens:* the needle points to the highest possible reading without a shadow of modesty or anxiety. For after all, Adler is a part of the human race.

I come full circle: the loss of revolutionary illusions, reality of the Gulag, oppression of the peoples of the Third World by their own governments have not abolished the iniquities and injustices in our liberal and democratic European community. The fate of *a shady-looking character* is merely an example of what is piling up in our backroom. We are all potentially an Adler or a Wallraff.

Translated from the Spanish by Lisa Wyant

RICHARD HOWARD

THE FOREIGNER
REMEMBERED BY A LOCAL MAN

Fuseli! I fancied the floor would tumble down—
could he be less than a giant, genius itself?
Footsteps approached, then a bony little hand

slid round the doorframe, followed presently
by a lion-faced, white-haired pygmy of a man
in a gown of old flannel gathered round his waist

by a length of rope, and wearing on his head
what I made out with some surprise to be
the bottom of Mrs. Fuseli's sewing basket . . .

My work was there. The Maestro stared about.
"By Godde," said he, "you will nefer paint finer.
It vas alvays in you, I haff said, and now,

by Godde, it is out! You haff de touch—it is
Wenetian entirely. But you look demn tin."
To such a point our converse fired him up

we drove instanter to Park Lane, the while
he swore like a fury—a very little one—
yet how relentless was his vehemence

as he strode among the marbles, filled with zeal:
"De Greeks vere goddes, goddes vere dey." It proved
a scene immortal in my sanguine life . . .

So far from London's smoke offending me,
it has always seemed sublime, a canopy
shrouding the City of the World. "By Godde,"

Fuseli said as we took the air that day,
"it is de smoke of Israelites making bricks."
"Grander, sir," said I: "it is the smoke

of a people who in freedom would have forced
the Egyptians rather to make bricks for them."
"Vell done, John Bull!" Fuseli cried aloud.

And now, this morning, Reynolds came: "He's gone."
"Who, sir?" "Fuseli." "A man of Genius . . ." "But
I fear of no principle." "Why, sir, say you so?"

"He has left, I hear, such drawings—quantities
shockingly indelicate." I had no heart
to finish my figure. Today must be a blank.

KATEB YACINE

ONE STEP FORWARD,
THREE STEPS BACK

▼▼

Winnie is waiting at a street corner.

WINNIE [*aside*]: He's not coming.

A man approaches her. He is wearing a driver's white dustcoat and visored cap. She draws back, then springs toward him.

WINNIE: Oh, it's you! In broad daylight! Right here in the center of town. And the cops are following you everywhere you go! That's a wonderful disguise. I didn't recognize you!

They kiss and go offstage. Winnie returns alone.

WINNIE [*aside*]: When we were married, he was on trial for treason. Every morning he had to be at the law courts in Pretoria, and I was living in Orlando. Most of the time he stayed nights in Pretoria to work on his defense with the other lawyers. He didn't even have time to have something to eat. I had to force him to. He was sitting down and starting to eat when the telephone rang. He had to leave to bail out somebody or another from a police station. While he was gone, I saw a string of people whose friends or parents were detained. He never had a chance to learn how committed I was. I never asked him if I should get involved in the women's demonstrations. The problem was that since he was not working anymore, my salary could only cover eating expenses. I knew I would lose my job if I demonstrated, but I did it anyway and I was arrested and fired even though I had been the first black social worker in the country. He never had a cent in his pocket. If he pleads two or three cases a day and if he's paid, he buys pretty dresses for our little girls. We live on fruits and vegetables. He says it's good for our health.

Nelson enters, and walks around the stage several times doing gymnastics, watched from a distance by a plainclothesman.

WINNIE [*aside*]: Always a cop shadowing him the minute he leaves the house. We've always lived on a tight budget. He's the one who chose our little bungalow. He was working for the Johannesburg city council. One day his boss at the department of works told him to choose a house, and he took a three-room one. He could have had a four-room one just next door, but that's the way he is. He wants the least pretentious things in life.

Finishing his exercises, Nelson rejoins Winnie, who gives him a vigorous rubdown.

WINNIE: You're off again?

NELSON: Yes, right away.

WINNIE: So I've come just to see you sweat.

NELSON: It's the only time I can see you.

A second cop crosses the stage and rejoins the first one.

WINNIE: They're watching me, too.

Nelson moves away.

WINNIE: You're going away?

NELSON: I'll take my cop along and leave you yours.

Nelson goes offstage, followed by the first cop, while the second cop circles around Winnie.

WINNIE [*aside*]: Well, there you have it, that's life. When my husband goes off, I still have my cop. Time to get back.

She goes and sits down on a bed. She is in her home, and no longer sees the policemen.

WINNIE [*aside*]: The last time he came to the house, there were a lot of people here and he asked me to put some things in a suitcase for him. He was standing outside the door and I couldn't get to him for all the people. I packed his travel bag and I wanted to hand it to him but he was gone. An hour later, someone came to pick up the bag. The next day

I learned from the papers that he had spoken to an assembly and I hadn't known a thing about it.

I had noticed that he was very quiet and doing a lot of thinking that week. One day, getting ready to wash his shirt, I noticed a receipt. He had paid the rent six months in advance, and that was a very unusual thing for him to do. I think he was trying to set my mind at ease. He was trying to make my life without him less worrisome. It was like that with the car. It wasn't working right. He took it in for fixing and left it for me at the garage. Oh, isn't he an angel. Maybe if I'd had a chance to get to know him better I would've found he had all kinds of faults. But there was only time to love him and long for him. I would wait at dawn for the sacred moment when he would tap on my window. I never knew when it would be. There never was a definite rendezvous. He'd come early in the morning for less than an hour. But later, when I was being watched day and night, it was up to me to get to him. Someone came by and told me to follow him in my car. We rode for a mile and stopped next to another car, which I got in. I never knew where I was. He had hiding places all over the country, most of them in the homes of whites. Then I heard he'd been arrested.

Winnie goes offstage. Nelson enters, surrounded by policemen. The court is announced, made up of three judges in black robes and white masks.

NELSON: First, I want to point out that my judges are white, and I am black. In order for the court to understand the state of mind that brings me here, I should recall my political antecedents, and attempt to shed light on the various factors that led to my actions. Many years ago when I was young, I listened to the old men of the tribe tell stories how it was in the good old days before the white man came. Our people lived in peace, and moved about the country freely and without fear. The land was ours. We were the masters of the fields and forests and rivers. The main resource was the land, and it belonged to the tribe as a whole. Private property didn't exist. There were no classes, rich or poor, and no exploitation of man by man.

This society still had many primitive and undeveloped elements, and would be unviable at the present time, but it did contain the seeds of democracy. I take a great interest in the organization of the first African societies, and they have been very much an influence on the development of my political ideas.

The court is aware that I am a lawyer. I have from the start of my career experienced difficulties owing to the color of my skin and my membership in the African National Congress. I could have law offices in the city only if I could obtain an authorization, which was denied. Later, I was granted a temporary waiver, but at the time of its expiration the authorities refused to renew it. They stated that my associate, Oliver Tambo, and I were to leave the city and practice in a native township, in a secluded place much too far away for our clients to come see us. That amounted to asking us to end our practice, to stop serving our countrymen and to lose the rewards for all our years of study. No self-respecting lawyer would have consented to do this. As a result we continued for several years to go on illegally occupying offices in town. All during this time threats of prosecution and expulsion were left hanging over our heads.

In the courts where we were practicing, many magistrates treated us with courtesy, but others treated us coldly, not to say with hostility. We knew that, however irreproachable our work, we could never dream of being named public prosecutor, deputy public prosecutor, or judge. We dealt with magistrates whose knowledge of the law and legal competence were no greater than our own, but whose superior position was a result of their white skin, and was protected by it.

Nine years ago, the Transvaal Law Society asked the Supreme Court to disbar me, owing to my part in the campaign against unjust laws. According to the Law Society, my actions in that campaign were inconsistent with the rules of conduct rightfully expected of the members of our honorable body. But on that occasion the Supreme Court declared that I had not overstepped my rights, that there was nothing discreditable in a lawyer's identifying himself with his people in their struggle for political rights, even if these activities violate the country's laws. The Supreme Court threw out the Law Society's request.

With a verdict in my favor, it was unthinkable that I would put an end to my political activities. But Your Honor may wonder why I thought it necessary to persist in the behavior that brought me into these difficulties, and also caused me to spend four years in the courts under indictment for high treason (before a verdict for acquittal) and several months in prison during the state of emergency declared in 1960 for the simple reason that the Government did not appreciate my views and activities.

We could not accept, at a time the regime was undergoing modifications, the possible continuance of the basic constitutional principle of white supremacy and domination, a principle that has brought the whole world's scorn down on South Africa and its constitution.

From the beginning our plan was to call for mass action only as a final resort, if the Government refused to listen and negotiate with us. But in that case we had decided to ask the people to go on strike, that is, not to show up at their places of work in the hope of bringing economic pressure to bear on the Government. We specified that the strike was to take place in an orderly fashion, and that we would ask people to remain in their homes.

Nevertheless, our campaign and our preparations soon provoked an artificial climate of revolution and civil war. I say "artificial"—deliberately sought—not by you, Your Honor, but by the Government who not only refused to listen to us and to have discussions with us, but decided to consider us dangerous revolutionaries disposed to violence

and disorder, impossible to bring to heel without the help
of overwhelming police forces and all legal or illegal coer-
cive means. It ordered the mobilization of the armed forces
so as to break up our peaceful protest by employing intim-
idation and terror.

The chief judge rings a bell.

CHIEF JUDGE: This session is adjourned.

REPORTER [*to audience*]: The local newspapers are saying the
strike was not observed. But I found the figures in the international press. In Johannesburg 40 to 75 percent of the
people went on strike. In Durban 50 percent of the Indian
workers stayed home, and in some places of business there
was 100 percent participation in the strike. Seventy-five percent of the nonwhite population of Port Elizabeth didn't go
to work, and of some five hundred nonwhite university students, less than fifty showed up for classes.

Nelson and the judge return face to face.

NELSON: The Government used the law to disrupt my personal
life, my career, and my political activity, in such a way as
to induce in me a profound contempt for the law. In December 1952, I was presented with a Government order, not
stemming from any judicial decision, but from pure and
simple high-handedness, or perhaps from a secret procedure. According to the terms of the order, I was not to go
outside the judicial district of Johannesburg for six months.
During this period I was forbidden to attend any public
meetings. These measures eventually expired, and three
months later, without the slightest respect for the right of
legal defense, without the least hint of contradictory procedure, these two interdictions were extended, this time
for a period of two years, and a third one was added: the
minister of justice ordered me to resign from the African
National Congress.

Toward the end of 1955 I found myself free to come and
go, but not for long. Starting in February 1956, the interdictions were extended—once again, by the administration,
not the judiciary—without deigning to listen to me, and for

a period of five years. Everywhere I went I was accompanied by police officers from the security service. In short, I was labeled a criminal—a criminal not found guilty. Under these conditions who would be surprised that a man soon becomes an outlaw?

It cost me a great deal of pain that I had to separate from my wife and children, to give up the joy of finding my family around the dinner table at the end of the workday, to choose to become a man constantly hunted by the police, and living apart from my loved ones in my own country.

I hate racial discrimination, and my hatred is strengthened because it is shared with the overwhelming majority of humankind. I hate the education that systematically inculcates children with race prejudice, and I hate all the more fiercely because I detest it together with millions of people around the world. I hate the pride that keeps the best part for a minority, and that reduces the majority to slavery. No punishment can make me hate any the less.

The chief judge rings his bell, and the courtroom empties. As the police lead Nelson away, demonstrators in the street shout his name, despite police charges.

DEMONSTRATORS: Carry on, Mandela!

REPORTER [*to the audience*]: As was expected, the tribunal sentenced Mandela to five years forced labor. The spectators in the courtroom joined with Mandela's supporters in the street, chanting: *"Tshotsholoza,* Mandela, carry on, Mandela!" The convicted man began serving his sentence at the Central Prison of Pretoria. He is in solitary confinement (twenty-three hours a day) and working at sewing mail sacks.

The reporter goes offstage. A loud noise is heard. Then a policeman's howl of pain. Two other policemen carry him off. Winnie is waiting for them with a shoe in her hand.

WINNIE: He barged into my house without knocking. He put his hand on my shoulder, talking gibberish. I didn't understand a word. If I'd had something in my hand I would have killed him.

FIRST POLICEMAN: It's serious. He's got a broken neck.

WINNIE: I was in the bedroom, my skirt hiked up, for God's sake, and this man came in without warning and didn't even excuse himself. He put his hand on my shoulder. I don't know what he did to land on the floor and break his neck. I grabbed him and knocked him over. I saw his legs fly out from under him, and I saw the chest of drawers fall over on him. He got what he deserved.

FIRST POLICEMAN: You'll have to tell your story at the station.

WINNIE: At least let me put my shoes on.

They roughly lead her away.

WINNIE [*aside*]: I am separated not just from my husband, but also from our two daughters. They had to attend so many different schools. They were expelled the minute it was found out who they were. Many times, they came back from school to find the house locked up. They had to get a newspaper to find out if I was in jail. And when I got out, I didn't have any work. I lost so many jobs . . . at a furniture store, a dry cleaner's, a shoe repairer's. I was hired on Monday and let go on Friday. One of my employers said, "You can keep this job for the rest of your life if you'll agree to get a divorce." He was told to say that by the police.

She goes offstage. The reporter enters.

REPORTER: Twenty thousand schoolchildren marched in the streets of Soweto to protest the government order to use only the language of the whites in black schools. Policemen and soldiers opened fire. Throughout the country blacks have responded by setting fire to schools, government buildings, state taverns, and motor vehicles. The South African Institute of Race Relations reported 618 dead and 1,500 wounded, most of them schoolchildren.

He goes off. Winnie comes back.

WINNIE [*to the audience*]: I was in Soweto and saw what happened. The children picked up stones, and held trash can lids as shields, and they walked up to the machine guns. I saw them die in the streets and, when they fell, others took their place. We couldn't stop our children. We couldn't keep them from going out on the streets. To defend them we formed the Black Parents' Association, and I went to the police station.

Enter Major Visser.

THE MAJOR: You organized the demonstrations, and now that you can't manage to keep them under control, you come to us. You realize, Winnie Mandela, that you are the cause of what is going on.

WINNIE: Child murderer! And you dare to say that we are the ones who organized the riots! Arrest this bastard who's killing our children in the streets!

She throws a shoe at his head. He leaves. A young policeman enters.

POLICEMAN: I am with the police and I too was in Soweto. You cannot imagine what it means to a chap my age to be forced to shoot on children because their skin color is different from mine. Even though I was ordered to fire point-blank, I want to assure you that I was careful to aim away. I didn't fire a shot.

They shake hands. The policeman goes offstage.

WINNIE: Our South Africa will be multiracial, and the government will be socialist.

She leaves. The reporter enters.

REPORTER [*to the audience*]: And so it begins again! Just a few months after his conviction, Mandela has just been taken from his cell with eight other detainees. They have been indicted for sabotage and conspiracy to overthrow the Government by revolution by becoming accomplices in a foreign invasion of South Africa. They are liable to the death sentence. Emotions are rising, both in this country and in the rest of the world.

Nelson is in the dock.

NELSON: I completely deny any involvement in any plan of sabotage.

On December 16, 1961, we attacked government buildings in Johannesburg, Port Elizabeth, and Durban. Our choice of these objectives reflected our policy. If we had wanted to make any attempt on human life, we would have aimed at objectives where people were collected, not empty buildings and power plants.

We were convinced the Government would react to the revolt by blindly massacring our brothers. It is just because our country's soil has already been stained with the blood of so many innocent Africans that we must get ready for a prolonged struggle in which force must be met with force. All the whites receive obligatory military training, no Africans. We had to form a nucleus of trained men who could direct operations.

We are accused of having the same aims as the communists. It is true that there often was close cooperation between the African National Congress and the Communist Party. I believe the communists have always played an active role in the struggle for freedom in colonized countries, because the short-term objectives of communism always correspond to the long-term objectives of liberation movements. When I was young, I thought that the admission of communists to the African National Congress, and the close cooperation between us and the communists—which occasionally occurred in connection with some particular problems—would end up changing the concept of African nationalism. I belonged to a group that demanded the expulsion of the communists from the African National Congress. The motion was voted down by a wide majority. Among those voting were some of the most conservative elements of African thought. They said that since its inception the African National Congress was not a party expressing rigorous political doctrine, but a forum of Africans that welcomed people of various political convictions but united in the common aim of national liberation. I was eventually converted to this view, and have maintained it from that time to the present.

Because of their anticommunist prejudices, South Africans may find it hard to understand how African political veterans so gladly accept communists as friends. But, to us, the reasons are clear. In our struggle against oppression, theoretical differences are a luxury that we cannot allow ourselves. Furthermore, for many decades the communists were the only South African political group who were prepared to treat Africans as humans, and thus as equals. They were ready to take their meals with us, talk with us, work with us. That is why today many of my countrymen equate communism with freedom, and they are confirmed in this belief by a body of laws that treats all supporters of freedom for Africans as communists, and that convicts a number of them—who are in fact not communists—on the basis of the law outlawing communism. Although never a Party member, I was hunted down as a communist. On the basis of this law, I was convicted, imprisoned, and banished.

The South African communists are, moreover, not the only ones who support us. The communist countries have always helped us. The basic task at the present time must be to eliminate all racial discrimination and to secure democratic rights. To the extent that the Communist Party pursues this objective, it will be welcome.

South Africa is the richest country on the continent, and could be one of the richest countries in the world. But it is a country of extreme contrasts. The whites enjoy possibly the highest standard of living in the world, while the Africans live in destitution.

Poverty goes hand in hand with illness and malnutrition. Nevertheless, the principal African complaint is less about being poor while the whites are rich than about the purpose of the laws passed by the whites, which is to maintain this situation. There are two ways to escape poverty: higher education with the awarding of officially recognized diplomas, and training in which the worker acquires greater skills in specialized work and so earns higher wages. For Africans, the law makes these two avenues of social advancement impossible.

Africans want wages on which they can live. We want to live where we find work, not to be expelled from some area on the pretext that we weren't born there. We want to have the right to own the lands on which we work. We want the freedom to mix with the general population, and not be confined to ghettos. The men want to have their wives and children nearby, where they work, and not be forced to live in camps reserved for men only. The women do not want to live like widows in the townships. Africans want the right to go out after eleven o'clock at night, the right to travel in their own country, and to look for work wherever they want. The ideal I have adopted is a democratic society. I hope to live to see it, but it is also an ideal for which I am ready, if necessary, to die.

A demonstration begins onstage, then goes off into the wings, and swings back again before President Botha comes onstage, followed by journalists.

CHORUS OF DEMONSTRATORS: Set Mandela free!

REPORTER [*to the audience*]: President Botha has put out a White Book. The Bible is no longer enough for the governing of South Africa. Blood is spilled every day, the prisons are full, and the demonstrators return to the charge.

DEMONSTRATORS: Set Mandela free!

BOTHA: Considering that influx control is no longer a constitutional objective, that basic rights must be protected, and that discrimination because of race or color is unacceptable, the government has decided to abolish influx control and to give top priority to the distribution of an identical document to all the groups in the population.

REPORTER: Influx control is a law that limits or suppresses free movement in a white area by requiring blacks over sixteen to have on them an internal passport so conceived that it has already permitted eighteen million blacks to be jailed. One arrest every three minutes!

DEMONSTRATORS: Set Mandela free!

REPORTER: Basically, nothing has changed. Segregation will remain the rule, and the same day this White Book was published, a bill was presented to the Parliament giving carte blanche to the forces of repression.

The reporter goes offstage. Three bankers enter.

FIRST BANKER: [*to Botha*]: So what is the Government doing? Looks like a failure! I'm here representing U.S. banks. Your debt to us now totals four billion two hundred million dollars.

SECOND BANKER: British banks claim three billion dollars.

THIRD BANKER: And you owe French banks two billion dollars.

BOTHA: Rest assured, gentlemen, that we have undertaken to institute important reforms.

DEMONSTRATORS: Set Mandela free!

FIRST BANKER: It is time to settle accounts. If you do not pay up, we will seize all your U.S. assets.

SECOND BANKER: Great Britain will do the same.

THIRD BANKER: And in France too, of course. Also Switzerland and other European nations.

FIRST BANKER: Let us recapitulate. You owe the Free World fourteen billion dollars.

BOTHA: Gentlemen, I beg of you! Listen to me. We are on the right track. The colonial system and the separation of the races are a thing of the past. I have spoken to the Parliament, on television, and in all the Sunday newspapers in a two-page spread. I addressed myself directly to the blacks. . . .

DEMONSTRATORS: Set Mandela free!

FIRST BANKER [*to Botha*]: And the blacks are responding.

SECOND BANKER: Set Mandela free.

THIRD BANKER: There's no more time to lose.

FIRST BANKER: If you don't wish to end up like the Shah, like Baby Doc, like Marcos.

DEMONSTRATORS: Set Mandela free!

The bankers exit.

REPORTER [*to the audience*]: Botha the Blockhead! The great bankers are furious with him. France has withdrawn its investments. The Security Council, the United States, the British Commonwealth have come out in favor of sanctions. And when the Chase Manhattan Bank refused to renew its loan of four hundred million dollars there was a panic. The South African rand was sold off to such an extent that the market fell. Forty-one U.S. firms have already pulled out. Sixty-three U.S. colleges and universities have withdrawn four hundred million dollars invested in South Africa. Inflation, lowered foreign exchange, a brain drain, and the flight of capital—this is the economic picture in a country where the level of unemployment has become critical. Of two and a half million unemployed, two million four hundred thousand are black.

DEMONSTRATORS: Set Mandela free!

Botha, overcome with worries, goes to sleep standing up by a wall at the back of the stage. In a dream he sees Mandela, who takes him by the hand, as if he were a little boy.

MANDELA: Still at the foot of the wall. Come, little Botha, I'll teach you how to walk. Come, go forward with me. One, two, three, four. You see? We've taken four steps. Now try and do it by yourself. Walk toward me. One . . .

Botha takes another step, but goes forward only to go backward, his back to the wall and his eyes closed.

MANDELA: Give me your hand. Forward, march!

Botha rubs his eyes as if blotting out a nightmare, and suddenly starts walking in a march step.

MANDELA: One, two, one, two . . .

BOTHA: Where are we going?

MANDELA: Halt! Stay like that. Above all, don't move. They're going to do a statue of you for the Museum of the Free World. Stand straight and hold your head up. Don't forget who you are. You'll be bringing in some dollars. You'll be sent off to America, to our Indian brothers, and you'll be shown off to the children in school, you, the superman.

Botha tries out a few becoming poses, but he is haunted by the chorus of demonstrators, like the worst nightmare.

CHORUS:

> I am black,
> I see all things in black,
> We are all black,
> Your world is black,

Our life is black,
Poverty, poverty black,
It is I the nigger,
I the half-caste,
I the Indian,
It's I who wash your window,
And I who wash your car,
And I who fall from your balcony,
Man white,
Man clean,
Man pink,
Man shiny
As a freshly minted penny,
It's you who live,
And I who croak,
It's we the intruders.
We who are from here!

Translated from the French by Franklin Philip

WILLIAM S. BURROUGHS

THE PARABLE
OF THE SILENT HEADS

⩡

This text is based on two newspaper accounts widely separated in time. . . . The first incident, circa 1950, took place in Mexico City. A campesino wearing cotton pants and shirt, rope sandals, with a machete at his belt, and a well-dressed businessman carrying a briefcase are waiting at a bus stop. The campesino, when questioned by the police, said:

"He kept giving me looks *muy feo* (very ugly) so that, finally, unable to contain myself, I drew my machete and cut his head off."

The second incident took place in Paris, 7:40 P.M., February 27, 1987.

Paris AP. A well-dressed man in his thirties drew a machete from his briefcase in a Paris subway station, slashed to death a drunken vagrant who was shouting insults and then strode away and vanished, police said Saturday. A police official said the killing occurred at 7:40 Friday in the busy Bastille metro station. The official, who spoke on condition of anonymity, said the vagrant was shouting general insults shortly before the killing.

Backdrop of Mexico City. A bleak, dusty street, newspapers in the wind. Two men stand at the bus stop. One is a well-dressed businessman in his thirties, carrying a briefcase. The other, a campesino weaving slightly. The businessman looks at his wristwatch and frowns. Still frowning he leans forward, looking up the street in the direction from which the bus will come. The campesino leans forward and looks at the businessman. . . . Lips peel back from his yellow buck teeth. His hair stands up . . . on end.

"CHINGOA!" he screams. Jerks out his machete and cuts the head off the businessman. The grimacing head bounces into the gutter and comes to rest against a crumpled newspaper. . . . Still clutching his briefcase, the headless body staggers spouting blood.

Cut to the Paris metro, Place de la Bastille . . . The campesino staggers around screaming curses. . . . Passengers walk by without a glance. . . . The vagrant focuses drunkenly on the businessman.

"WHAT are you looking at?"

The businessman stops. Reaches into his briefcase and pulls out a machete. Holding the case in his left hand he slashes through the vagrant's throat to the spine. Calmly he replaces the machete . . . and walks up the subway stairs into a backdrop of Mexico City. . . . He disappears into the street of the beginning scene.

NTOZAKE SHANGE

PASSAGES: EARTH SPACE

For Nelson Mandela and the Children of Azania

there is no one in the bottom of a champagne bottle
there's no guerrilla waiting with loaded uzi
     to sail down the san juan river
     gunning for *commandante zero*
there's no one to help me free nelson mandela
     or bring the *murderers* of victoria mandela
     to their rightful brutal deaths

the bottom of a champagne bottle is a pitiful
     American gesture / celebrating dishonestly
the will to die for freedom
     outside durban or capetown

for south african blacks / champagne is *verboten*
     (too good for the dirty kaffirs) *Azanians*

When the ANC marches over botha's
     dried & hate-filled bones / his sinews
     crippled with wickedness / mauled under
     the feet of children whose lives he'd have

wiped out / if it weren't for the mines / diamonds
     & gold / he imagines his skeleton shines
     like gold / his skull on a ray of diamonds /
mind you / he's being crushed as he would
crush angola / as he imagines cabral is silenced /

botha banned
   the marching feet of millions of children
another way to free nelson mandela / to
ban krugerrands as the israelis would obliterate
palestines & mengeles /
     no questions asked / only the skin as evidence
  of heinous crimes or innocence /
wisdom / there are no freedom fighters armed /
  & ready / chanting

PATRIA O MUERTE

NICARAGUA VENCIA / EL SALVADOR VENCERA
   que viva la liberación de la gente negra
    del africa del sur
    namibia
     angola
      grenada
       mozambique
  quien sabe donde estará / el próximo
    territorio libre / no solamente en américa
pero en el mundo /

PATRIA O MUERTE

que viva la liberación mundial
  une vie sans oppression
    pour toi / para ti / une vie sans
  oppression /
   where the color / the color of our
   skin is not evidence of heinous
crimes or innocence.

ADONIS

LIKE A FIELD OF LOVE

No road leads to where he lives
everything is under siege—the streets a graveyard
but far away, above his house,
a roving moon
grasped
in strands of dust.

Let him keep his secrets
now he sets the sea in his guts
now he sets it at his window
let him keep his secrets
disguise himself as a bud
clothe the face with a stone
let him keep his secrets
like a field of love
that each season metamorphoses
and leafs the trees

He knows birds
that perch on their voices
and fly with branches

The farthest light
is nearer than
the nearest dark

distance
a myth
probably

The massacre changed the image of the town
this stone a child's head
this smoke
men's breath

Birds refuse to sing
in fields where silence is unknown

OLYMPE
BHÊLY-QUÊNUM

MASHOKA ELFU MOJA
(THE THOUSAND AXES REBELLION)

▼▼

I begin to find an idle and fond bondage in the oppression
of aged tyranny; who sways, not as it hath power, but as it
is suffered. (*King Lear*, I, ii)

We have seen the best of our time: machination,
hollowness, treachery, and all ruinous disorders, follow us
disquietly to our graves. (*King Lear*, I, ii)

*My friend Blaise Senghor was the first person to read this novella,
which he hoped to make into a film about "independent Africa" and
which I am allowing to be published as a contribution to the struggle
of Nelson Mandela. Unfortunately, Senghor's death intervened to
prevent him from carrying out this project.*

Old Anikokou smiled with his eyes. The senior maker of
edged tools in Alfajiri had come up with a few modifications
in the traditional implements: a solid cast-iron head with a
light or shorter handle, or a lighter or thicker head than before, but fitted with a handle that was shorter and less heavy.

At first, the other members of the guild had protested vehemently, and the purchasers, too. But the users decided the
changes were for the better, since the tools seemed handier
and more functional. Later the same toolmakers who had criticized Anikokou confessed, "If we didn't tell you, we would
be wrong and the gods would look upon us unfavorably."

"Fear of the gods—an important sentiment—is characteristic of the sons of Alfajiri who have a care for their country's progress," said old Anikokou.

After the evening meal, the delegation of former apprentices who had come to the reconciliation—though there hadn't been any actual rift between him and them—followed him with their hands behind their backs and their heads slightly bowed. Anikokou walked with the bearing of a tranquil man who had dealt with many problems and on whom nothing was pressing. He and his confreres were going to sit beneath the kapok tree in Ilé-Imo's village square, on a horizontal tree trunk supported by three thick forked posts in the ground—which had served for generations as a bench. The group chatted till late in the night. The eminent craftsman loved his trade; he had taught some three hundred young men in Alfajiri, and many of the local blacksmiths came to him for consultation. Hoes, axes, hatchets, arrows, picks, knives, or machetes from his smithy and those of his former apprentices carried a barely perceptible guild mark distinguishing them from tools made by anyone other than those "marked with the stamp of old Anikokou."

He had reflected a good deal, and taken counsel with the gods before instituting the modifications. Tall, slender, seemingly frail, with sharp eyes in a bony face, Anikokou had nappy, graying hair, and a salt-and-pepper goatee which he instinctively stroked with the fingers of his left hand as he talked. The *adire* loincloth with which he draped himself, leaving the right side of his body bare to his waist, suited him. He also wore a full *cãká* with spurs of indigo-blue velvet, a kind of longish shorts pegged below the knee.

His judicious comments, like his great craftsmanship, added to his reputation throughout Ilé-Imo. The markets of Alfajiri were increasingly filled with agricultural equipment from Europe and other "villages of the whites," though not yet altogether deterring the peasants and locals from domestic production. But old Anikokou had a good nose, for he sensed the threat, and after seeking counsel from the gods, he envisioned little modifications in all the locally produced tools. While he worked, he liked to hum songs about great historical events featuring gods and ancestors. One day when his nephew Noupko was staying with him during the school vacation, Anikokou was stimulated by the tune he was murmuring, and he abruptly left his workshop, holding the hatchet he had been working on. He bounded out into the compound courtyard where a great oleander tree cast a deep and restful shadow. There he performed three strategic dance steps, paused, laid the hatchet on the ground, and tightened the sash of his many-pleated pants with their wide, deep pockets. Then he picked up the tool and began a war dance.

A thousand memories swirled in his head. Had he not at the age of fifteen taken part in the fight between Ilé-Imo and the village of Fissilè, which was utterly defeated and forced to disappear? Anikokou wielded the hatchet, now a weapon of war, brandished it over his head, charged the retreating enemy, and faced the brave ones; then the weapon soared off and struck the fleeing man at more than fifty yards or drove hard into the brave one determined to resist.

Noupko admired him, and loved his joy, his tact, his limitless fund of Alfajirian history. All of a sudden, the old man stopped dancing. He had realized the hatchet could be improved. He studied the device, feeling the iron and patting the handle head, then darted back into his workshop and worked there until late.

The next day he showed his nephew both the old and new hatchets. They left the compound for the open space in front of the house. Noupko hefted both tools, then sprang ten paces forward, then one step back. His uncle smiled at his rough, citified imitation of a war dance, but Noupko brandished the old hatchet and sent it hurtling at a tree some fifty yards away. It hit the mark. Then he took the new one, swung it around over his head and with the same effort he had used before, sent it farther than the first one.

"This one works better. It's got a heavier head. And the handle's shorter. It goes like lightning," said Noupko.

"You're a true son of an edge-tool maker," said Anikokou with pride. He added that the new model had been used in the fight of the people of Ilé-Imo against the miserable aggressors from Fissilè.

"Now I realize there would have been a lot more killing if we'd had hatchets like this, which go faster and come closer to the mark."

But there was no more fighting between villages. Alfajiri had become a free country, governed by its own indigenous people. The whites, who had once been in control and had seized the "brawlers," beaten them, and thrown them into prison, were forced to yield to the men they called the "new masters." And the new masters did not tolerate any violation of the new laws.

"All right, so long as they don't keep us from using our own things."

"It'll come to that. The other day, I mean the market day in Kisse, they were screaming over the radio that no one must be against progress."

"Yes, and the guy kept using what the children call 'big words.' They seemed to be talking mainly to us peasants."

"You must not be misoneists; you must accept European techniques and technology, which bring civilization even to the villages that are the farthest from urban centers," the minister of information had shouted on the radio.

A journalist had translated the speech into the national languages, but the translations had been confused, throwing the peasants from considerable obscurity into total darkness.

"The way they talk, those guys manage to make us foreigners in our own languages."

Noupko had to explain the remarks of the acculturated minister, who was unable to speak any of the national languages without making mistakes. Like many other "fattened ministerial animals," rigmarole French—always badly translated—was his only means of communication with an illiterate

populace who consequently did not understand their political
leaders.

"What? Those snotnoses think we peasants are afraid of
progress and things that are new?"

"Really? We had no civilization, and wouldn't have until
the whites came?"

"Tell me, little one, what do they mean by civilization?"

"I think they were born among the whites and they are
living here like exiles."

The evening was moonlit. Noupko loved to take part in the
chatter under the tall kapok tree in the village square. He had
come to absorb the avuncular wisdom and affection of Anikokou.

Directly on his return from Ilé-Imo to Shoka, the country's
political and economic capital, Noupko was as though
snatched up and tossed into unprecedented turmoil. A strike
launched by the Pupils' and Students' General Union para-
lyzed the whole of Alfajiri from the end of the rainy-season
vacation. The vice chancellor, like the academic inspector,
first spoke about the "sudden change of mood displayed by
some spoiled children and anarchists." But the unrest lasted
for three weeks. Now and then the radio, which was controlled by the revolutionary government, broadcast like a leit-
motiv: "Well, these students and pupils, who have everything
they need to be content, are still refusing to go back to class."

In a lengthy diatribe and rhetorical tour de force, later
printed in *The National Awakening,* Alfajiri's lone daily, the minister of education, Idowu Ologbo, stigmatized "the strikers
and intellectuals, stuffed with poorly assimilated foreign ide-
ologies, who are incapable of saying what they mean and what
they expect of their country's revolutionary, democratic, and
progressive government."

It happened after a meeting of the council of ministers.
The twenty-five members of the "plethoric government" had
been sitting for fifteen hours without a break. The director of
the radio, Odunlami Majoou, termed this council "a shameful

punishment inflicted on the worthy, devoted, and understanding leaders who have, like the paternal compatriot and chief of state, General Mahoro Tonoudouto himself, been obliged to take a lunch and dinner of sandwiches."

The council chamber was a large room over a thousand feet square, the walls covered with locally produced red linen spangled with gold. Thirty tooled-bronze bracket lamps, all the same height, were affixed to the walls, in the form of flowers in bloom, a half-opened hand, or two hands severed or tightly clasping and chained to wrists, the heads of reptiles or gargoyles spitting fire or blood, even penises and vaginas whose eerie realism startled even the dullest minds when the electric lights went on. The ceiling, stretched with fabric of old gold encrusted with images of African flora and fauna, had a ten-inch-wide frieze of sculpted teak set at right angles to it.

Closer inspection of this masterpiece, the product of eighteen months' work by the guild of old sculptors, revealed the national history, the bases of education and traditional religious symbols, onto which were grafted images of the daily lives of the common people. From the ceiling hung three eighteenth-century bronze chandeliers from Europe, each weighing more than a hundred pounds. The floor was composed of twelve-inch squares of pale pink marble decorated with discreetly erotic pastoral scenes or scenes of daily life made up of red, green, black, yellow, and brown mosaic tiles.

The solid mahogany table measured twenty-four feet long and six feet wide. Its ten feet were sculpted into lions' paws with claws drawn, standing on an opulent Persian carpet thirty-six feet long and twelve feet wide. A red cloth covered the table. Generalissimo Tonoudouto's government was going through a critical period, though there was still hope of bringing it to an end.

The chief of state rose and took a meditative stroll around the table. Tall, muscular, robust, large-bellied and broad-bottomed, he had been a warrant officer in Europe at the time his country became independent. An illiterate peasant conscripted into the colonial troops in 1938, he had profited from his being stationed in Europe by acquiring some education and culture. The contacts among the black students he met enabled him to learn, after the war, about the problems facing the peoples of Africa.

Passably intelligent, but a plodder, he picked up ideas about law, economics, and political science. A barracks mate lent him a book, *Selected Readings in Marxism-Leninism;* another friend with whom he stayed while on leave gave him a copy of *The Bases of Liberal Economics.* After devouring both books, Tonoudouto developed an interest in *The Foundations of Mathematics,* and also literature, not in "very old" authors, but in those of the nineteenth and twentieth centuries. He found their eloquence and their denunciatory analyses of social crises stimulating. His contacts with the African students also encouraged him to read African writers and "subversive" journalists.

On Tonoudouto's return to Shoka, he quickly sized up his superior officer, found him rough and intellectually uncultivated, but the ideal military man. He was educated and had even acquired a form of political strategy noticeably absent in the captains, lieutenants, and lieutenant colonels spontaneously born of national independence. Mwasherati, then chief of state, was a former expeditionary clerk—tall, portly, with heavy jowls and an intelligent gaze. Weak and sensual, coddled by a circle of "European technical counselors," he found Tonoudouto quite shrewd and pliant, and made him his chief of staff.

Eight months later, an internal shake-up in the Presidential Palace of the Republic soon turned into a power struggle, which degenerated into a coup d'état.

In the confusion Tonoudouto dispatched Mwasherati with a knife straight to the heart. Following this Brutus-like act, he plunged into the crowd, weeping hot tears, in pursuit of "whoever had so pusillanimously taken the life of the Nation's Father, a man loved, even adored, by all his fellow citizens."

Then he quickly took over the government, claiming a fuller understanding than anyone else of the ideas and "philosophy" of Mzee Mwasherati. To the great surprise of the people, who loudly decried the dictatorship and misadministration, all the superior officers from Camp Kinimandjè kept silent, and kowtowed to their mess comrade, who was determined to respond with arms after having demobilized them all. Without further ado and in less than three days the world's chiefs of state recognized Alfajiri's new chief of state. And no one in the country mourned Mzee Mwasherati. Many criticized him, pointing out his character of a *sulafi** and an *anas nyingi,*† and condemning his "misappropriation of public funds."

Two years after seizing power, Mahoro Tonoudouto was surrounded with "boyhood pals" and "barracks mates." The very words used to accuse Mwasherati and his now-imprisoned "power clique" again began to circulate. Worse—a student, Kwamé Séguè'ndé, had printed and distributed a pamphlet entitled *Reign of the Greedy Jackals* containing sayings of Chairman Mao, who was, however, uncredited by name. Tonoudouto fell into the trap, and spoke of a "handful of students and troublemakers guilty of subversive and intolerable writings and who must be punished without pity." A short time later, when the Radio of the Progressive and Military Democratic Revolution was airing this glaring proof of ignorance and lack of culture, a dozen cars with fake license plates sped through the city dropping broadsides with Mao's sayings but this time with quotation marks and giving the author's real name.

"General, the sayings that your excellency attributed to schoolkids were those of Great Comrade Mao Tse-tung himself."

"Arrest Captain Akoutou, and jail him for fifteen days! He has called me an ignoramus!" shouted Tonoudouto, beside

*glutton
†voluptuary

himself with anger, his face hard and his hands and neck streaked with blood-swollen veins.

"Generalissimo! Excellency! I never said that!" protested Akoutou.

"You thought it!" said the chief of state.

"Never! As God is my witness! Forgive me, Generalissimo."

"You spineless son of a bitch! Fifteen months in jail. And if you open your mouth again, I'll have your wife Mji brought in and I'll screw her before your very eyes before I have you locked up."

Captain Akoutou felt as though he were lying in a grave. He was of medium height, pleasingly muscled, with fine features and a veil of stupidity and cowardice constantly playing over his face. Tonoudouto ordered him taken to the military prison and at the same time demanded "the pursuit and immediate arrest of the hoodlums who are scattering inflammatory tracts around the country."

Like a fishnet on the high seas, fifty black police cars, sirens blaring, fanned out through the city. The alarms threw the "distributors of shameful papers" into a panicked run.

"It's no joke! It's a hunt for political miscreants!"

"Bunch of bastards and usurpers!"

"Neocolonialists! Murderers!"

"Absolute murderers. They've got death on our trail!"

They ran faster, used the poorest streets, throwing fistfuls of broadsides over the red-soil fences around houses, shouting that terror and death were looming over Alfajiri.

"THE KILLERS IN POWER WANT TO SILENCE THE YOUNG PEOPLE! PARENTS OF ALFAJIRI, ACT QUICKLY!"

Some jumped from a car which they abandoned, scurried into the bush, and vanished. Heading for the outskirts, the police vans ran down five students and dragged their bodies for a hundred yards, their heads smashed open, rib cages crushed, limbs and sex organs torn off, but still convulsively jerking.

One "truncheon man" felt his vehicle hit something. He leaned out, saw the damage and the car spattered with blood, and coldly concluded: "Bunch of subversive jerks. There's no cause to declare national mourning."

Several distributors of "filthy and pernicious broadsides" were cornered, beaten, and thrown into the "animal cages" where they were tortured or subjected to other indignities. Abiodun, Wlanvie, and Utamu were among those apprehended by car number 7895. The cops frisked them, exchanged a few whispers, and then drew lots. Then Corporal Ubaya seized Abiodun, an economics student, knocked her down and put his knee on her chest, keeping his arms crossed. The corporal had a solid, steatopygous body with a spongy face and sensual lips. He sweated struggling against this twenty-year-old woman, slender, lithe, pretty, and surprisingly resistant.

"Go to it, chief!" said Ubaya, who then commented, gasping with hate: "The chief is going to fuck you, you little cow. When you get your ass fucked, you'll know better than to fuck with the established order and the authorities!"

Sergeant Mende, as ugly as his colleague, but lean and spider-faced, tore off Abiodun's *adire* cloth skirt and panties. The other two "agitators"—seated on two benches, in handcuffs, with their feet crossed and tied—looked on powerless at this scene of brutality and humiliation. Neither moved. Two black ferocious-looking German shepherds sat by each bench, keeping the students in check. An occasional growl was followed by short barks. One dog got up, took a few steps, and directed his muzzle toward Abiodun's sex.

"Not for you, Caïd, but watch her. If she makes a fuss, I'll give her to you and you can chew her clitoris."

Sergeant Mende liked a situation to be clear. He was supposed to be a personal friend of the chief of state and was feared by his subordinates, as well as more than a few of his superiors. He unbuttoned the fly of his dark green trousers and brought out a large tumescent sex. Abiodun, pinned to the ground by Ubaya who was on his knees next to her head, saw the obscene appendage. Reflexively, she crossed her legs and thighs.

"Disgusting!"

"Depraved! Obscene!"

"You're using a degrading and criminal situation to live out your fantasies!"

"And that's in charge of national security," said the students, immobilized on the bench.

Already up on their paws, the two German shepherds began to growl menacingly. One barked three times and the fur rose around his powerful neck.

"The dogs tell you the answer without us telling them to, that's all you're worth, jerks!" said Ubaya.

"Don't get complicated. If you're still a virgin—and I'll bet not—I'm going to deflower you. If you like strong sensations, fight me and I'll rape you so hard you'll scream. But by all the gods, don't make me lose patience!" said the sergeant, not bothering to respond to his colleague's retorts.

He used his hands, on which he wore ritual iron or copper coiled rings, to press violently on Abiodun's thighs, who cried out and uncrossed her legs. The Defender of the National Security thrust himself in the space created and got straight into action. Abiodun gesticulated wildly.

"Now let go of her arms. I want to take her to paradise all by myself," said the panting sergeant.

He grasped the sweating and screaming girl's arms.

"Hold still! You're not a virgin and too much fuss'll cost you. Caïd, watch her. She's starting to piss me off with all this twitching."

The dog got up and took up a spot near Abiodun's head. She cried out in terror seeing his muzzle too close to her face. The dog growled and bared its fangs. Abiodun let out a long sigh. Her nerves relaxed. She felt like death. At that instant the sergeant's sex organ went deep into her. Then he truly looked like a roach. Abiodun yelled for help. Her eyes turned up, her mouth open in a daze, her lips dripping with saliva and her tongue hanging out as if she had been garroted with a slip knot. Her outraged but helpless comrades wept in loud sobs, as though they were losing the dearest thing in the world. Undeterred, Sergeant Mende went on copulating until the cork popped, letting the flux run out in jerks. Exhausted and broken, Abiodun sobbed as much from pain as from being treated as a convenient hole.

The sergeant felt no further resistance and withdrew, but then he spotted blood on the floor and bloodstains on his fly.

"You dirty bitch! You could've told me you were on the rag!"

"You've . . . you've torn me and devirginized me." She began crying.

"Virgin! Aren't you ashamed to be a virgin, you silly cunt!" said Mende, bursting out laughing.

"Let's see if you too say you're untouched," said Ubaya, pawing at Wlanvie's breasts. She spat in his face.

The corporal slapped her hard enough to send her flying. Her nose started bleeding, and she coughed up blood.

"Murderers! Murderers! Murderers!"

"Killer of young people!"

"Cuckolds! And you take it out on our girls!"

"Butchers of the people!" chanted the students, who had decided to risk their lives.

"Shut up, or I'll set the dogs on you!" ordered the sergeant, seeing Caïd and Ajà in attack position, fangs bared.

"Race of pigs!"

"Race of imperialists!"

"Race of criminals!" shouted the students in unison, clomping their bound feet.

One was shouting louder than the others. Ajà sprang on him.

"Stop, Ajà!" ordered Ubaya. The dog froze, its forepaws on Nguki's chest and about to bite him in the face.

There was a deathly silence. Ajà backed away, growling.

"Now I'm going to ball you doggy-style," taunted Ubaya, undoing the rope around Wlvanie's feet and removing her handcuffs.

He then took off her clothes without encountering much resistance. Naked, Wlanvie hung her head, her hands crossed over her sex which was lost in a fleece of black hair, and she quietly wept. She was a woman of medium height and a sculpted body with fine firm breasts and softly rounded buttocks.

"Certainly, you too, no man will've screwed you before me," said Ubaya, taking a long prospective look at her body.

"If that's what's bothering you, you didn't have to take my clothes off."

"Watch it, you little cunt! I said I was going to ball you. *Secundo,* I asked you a question. Answer me."

"You didn't ask me anything," replied Wlanvie, and added dryly, "I used to go to school with your daughter Fimilé. If she isn't a virgin, I'm free to be one or not."

The corporal gave her another slap. He did not appreciate her mentioning his daughter, who had become pregnant at fifteen and had had a miscarriage two days after her father had given her a strenuous beating. Viassin, the young man accused of "lack of respect" for the corporal's daughter, was expelled from Tunuka College. He, too, had been involved in the protest against the established order.

"Whore! You little tart! Get on all fours!" shouted Ubaya.

"I am not an animal!" cried Wlanvie.

"Yes, you are! You're a bitch and I'm going to fuck you doggy-style!"

"No! No! Don't! Do anything, but not that!" she cried, haggard, suddenly realizing the humiliation the corporal was about to force on her.

"I order you to get on all fours! Got it?"

Wlanvie fell to her knees—emptied, pitiable, her wild eyes going from one comrade to the other. Both looked at her helplessly.

"You'll do it tomorrow, maybe? Watch it, you little whore, I'm going to get mad!" warned Ubaya.

Wlanvie complied. Her friends lowered their eyes to the sight of her naked flesh. Ubaya unbuttoned his pants and let them drop. But to his surprise the tension fell, his sex retracted and drooped. Flustered, panicky, the corporal clasped his genitals and began masturbating, yelling, "You slut! You witch! I'll kill you! You've put a spell on me!"

Forgetting their plight for a second, the students started to laugh. The dogs imposed silence with furious barking. Ubaya yanked his belt from his pants and vigorously whipped the back and buttocks of Wlanvie, who, crying out, remained as if nailed in her bestial position.

The current came back on. The corporal's sex became threatening, and in an attack of hate he took Wlanvie, who gave a sharp cry. Ajà and Caïd came up in front of the victim.

"Show her how only cops really know how to make her come," said the sergeant, looking at his colleague and rubbing his fly, while Ubaya fornicated with the girl with all the fury of a hopeless impotent in whom the current has miraculously switched on, but only for a short while.

When Ubaya withdrew his blood-covered sex, Wlanvie collapsed, her face on the floor, spread-eagled as though crucified on her stomach.

"Who gets to fuck this other bitch?" asked Mende. At these words Utamu, who no longer felt alive, fainted. All of them were frightened, including the torturers, so none of them blamed his penis for this.

On the orders of Ku-Chinja, minister of the interior, the insurgents were brought to the President of the Republic.

"Scum! Hoodlums! Would-be intellectuals! Bunch of hemorrhoidal assholes!" General Tonoudouto foamed with rage, walking in circles around them.

He halted abruptly, and looked at them in surprise, as if he had just noticed the young people's bodies, which had been beaten, humiliated, and knocked to the ground in the sun. Then he called them low filthy little guttersnipes collared by the police, and burst into noisy laughter that shook his whole body.

"What do we do with them, general?"

"A hundred lashes with the *chicotte* for each one of these vermin," cried the chief of state.

"A hundred smart strokes of the *chicotte*, then throw them in prison," the minister ordered Omonaja, a police sergeant standing at attention.

"Two of our comrades were raped in a police van by Corporal Ubaya and Sergeant Mende," said Amouzou.

At these words General Tonoudouto strode up to this "shameless cockroach" and spat in his face.

"Pity there aren't any queers among my honorable guardians of the peace. I'd gladly ask him to butt-fuck you to death!" declared the chief of state.

The sun was setting over the town like an incandescent boiler. The "disturbers and phony revolutionaries" were led to the courtyard of the presidential palace, where a tall kapok tree, three jacarandas, three eucalyptuses, two tall acarpous fig trees, coconut palms, mango and other fruit trees cast a deep shadow. The insurgents looked at each other questioningly.

"If I weren't neutralized this way, I'd kill myself."

"Not me. They beat me, you won't even hear a whimper."

"That should be the policy for every one of us."

"But that'd make them mad. They could kill us."

"They might do that anyway. See those dogs over there?"

"So do we stand up to them?"

"Okay, it's a deal. Promise?"

"Promise!"

A bundle of green, stout, flexible *chicottes* were brought out, and the police got to work. The whistling rods came down and bit into the students' flesh. They had been made to strip naked, except for the girls, who kept the strict minimum. But the blood and sperm-oozing panties of the two girls who had been raped were a repellent sight compounded by a swarm of flies collecting around the pubic areas. The guardians of the peace flailed the "disrespectful young people" with all their might, but no one cried out, even though blood flowed down their backs and down their legs. Some urinated, some even defecated, but all of them kept their mouths closed and gritted their teeth and not a tear spilled from their red, pain-filled, but dry eyes.

The guardians of public order declared this stoicism a "fool's resistance." Then they grew bolder until they ran out of breath, unused to such hard work in less than a working day.

"I'm thirsty," moaned Almohade.

"I'm gonna piss in your mouth," responded a cop, bringing down more blows.

A sudden cry went up. *"Maito. Maito! Thaaaaaai!"*

Then the cry faded into a stunned silence. It was Nguvu. His maternal grandmother was a Kikuyu who had emigrated to Tanganyika, where Nguvu had lived to the age of eighteen before coming to Alfajiri.

"Maito. Maito. Thai." Mother. Mother. Peace.

Forgotten words from his childhood rose up from the deepest part of him. Now he stirred no more. General Tonoudouto, seated in a red leather armchair, was observing the operation from the lobby where he had withdrawn. He had been struck by the passivity of the insurgents and had called them "nihilists." But after Nguvu's cry he was forced to intervene.

"Stop!" he ordered.

The lashing ceased, and it was seen that one of the students was dead. Tonoudouto was dismayed, and the policemen were shouting insults, calling the body a "filthy crab louse."

"He pulled a suicide. Get rid of the body, and let's have no more talk about this," decreed Alfajiri's chief of state.

"That's not true. It wasn't a suicide. You murdered him," shouted Wlanvie, bursting into tears.

All the rebels began weeping loudly. The body of their comrade Nguvu, scored all over from the blood-dripping *chicottes*, lay on the ground in the peaceful shade, his gaze fixed and his mouth gaping in surprise, his lips drawn back to reveal his firmly implanted white teeth.

"Water them down with buckets of water. That'll calm their nerves. Then stick 'em in jail and forget all this crap," ordered General Tonoudouto.

The bodies of the students run over by the vans of the "forces of order" were deposited with their parents. The grieving families left the town by night, taking their children's remains back to their villages for burial. They wanted to avoid bringing the attention of the authorities, not on their misfortune, but on themselves. If the chief of state knew who the victims' parents were, he would have them spied on and ask that anything they said be reported to him, which would be zealously done, with interpretations.

The precautions of the parents of Afiwa, Mimuni, Messan, Yessuf, Latif, and Nguvu—casualties of General Tonoudouto's repressive government—persuaded a group of students who had escaped that day's institutionalized barbarity to make some suggestions to the cruelly tried families. Another event added to their embitterment. Reports came that the young people in jail had revolted. The rumor had brought false reports to Tonoudouto's ears. He loved to pick up information, and with this in mind he sometimes disguised himself and went out at night alone driving a pearl gray Fiat A26. The general wanted to get precise details about this "rabble-rousing." He summoned the minister of the interior, Ku-Chinja, to his office.

"That is not quite correct, your excellency. Sergeant Mende, whom I called in as soon as I learned about these rumors, confirmed that they came down to some agitator eating his own excrement," said Ku-Chinja.

"What? A human being who treats himself to a dinner of shit?" cried the chief of state. The minister stifled a giggle.

"The kid is like a trained dog, general. They told him 'evacuate,' and he did it right on the spot. Then they said, 'eat it,' and he began eating what he had evacuated."

"That's incredible! That's phenomenal! I've got to verify this *de visu*," decided the general.

Sergeant Mende and his adjutant were on a mission to the town of Yake, where the repression of a clash had ended in a bloodbath. So it fell to the jailer Githunguri—tall, strong, thick-set, head shaved daily—to show the chief of state how well he had trained the young prisoner Makaburini.

Githunguri had large black piercing eyes, a sensual mouth, and an abundant and carefully groomed mustache. For some reason he didn't like Makaburini, taking an aversion to him the second day of his imprisonment. One day he beat the young man until the blood flowed, and the poor wretch relieved himself in his pants. Shocked by this "lack of decency and cleanliness," Githunguri commanded Makaburini Uhalifu to eat all that filth, all of it immediately. And, as though he had been asked to perform some natural habitual act, Makisha, as he was familiarly called, began eating his feces. Githunguri burst out laughing. He invited a few colleagues to see a one-of-a-kind event, and they crowded around to see the young man docilely ingesting his own feculence.

The next day, without any preliminary belt-lashing, but now in the presence of his superiors, Githunguri gave peremptory orders to the young prisoner, who promptly lowered his ragged urine-stained pants, squatted, and defecated.

"What a stench!" commented Githunguri's superiors, pinching their nostrils.

"Eat!" shouted the jailer, and the student got to work.

"Oh, by the gods! He's crazy!" said the jailer's superiors, averting their dumbfounded gazes.

When General Tonoudouto came to the jail with his minister of the interior, Githunguri had his victim led into the yard, to the base of a magnificent, fragrant jacaranda in flower. In rags, disheveled, his face long and cadaverous, Makaburini shuffled forward apprehensively, head down and shoulders hunched.

"It seems you fill your pants?"

"Yes ... yes ... gene ... ge ... general," the young man stammered.

"It seems you're a coprophage?"

Githunguri, who didn't know the word, was surprised, and he looked questioningly at the student, who answered, "Yes ... yes ... gene ... ge ... general."

"Why you little devil, why do you do that?"

"The ... the ... chief Githungur ... jail ... jailer ... a ... a ... asked me to."

"Is this true, Githunguri?"

"Yes, your excellency," answered the jailer, standing at attention.

"Well, I want to see it," said the general, dubious.

"Let your pants down!" ordered the jailer.

Makaburini promptly complied, and stood naked, his penis shrunken and wrinkled.

"Defecate!" said Githunguri sharply.

Makisha slowly squatted and got going.

"Now, eat!"

The student scooped up a handful of the fearsome, stinking hash, but instead of peacefully putting it to his lips, as he had done each time Githunguri demanded, he abruptly heaved the disgusting stuff in General Tonoudouto's face. There was a wondrous uproar, followed by a lightning-fast response. From somewhere came a shot, and Makisha silently crumpled to the ground with his face in his own blood and excrement.

Some of the frantic onlookers got out their handkerchiefs, others took off the jackets of their uniforms, and others even tore their shirts to wipe the face and fancy parachutist's uniform of the desecrated chief of state. But in the hubbub of men stricken with fear and distress, another pistol shot rang out. Githunguri screamed, and then he, too, toppled over. It was seen that General Tonoudouto—stiff, his face smeared—was still clutching his pistol.

The general was a crack shot. He mumbled a few curses,

and hastily retreated to his armored limousine, a black Mercedes, which roared off, though the noise was drowned by the clamor of motorcycle sirens.

News of Generalissimo Tonoudouto's double murder spread quickly in Shoka and soon reached every part of Alfajiri. Makaburini's murder fired the students' determination to the point of paroxysm. The young people, whom the chief of state had branded as spoiled children and nihilists in five radio broadcasts in two weeks, began telling their murdered comrades' parents about their country's economic, political, and social situation.

"Our mothers' and sisters' once-flourishing business activities used to add to this country's reputation. Now, no more female tradespeople. All the saleswomen of cloth, thread, and locally produced crafts products have gone to live in neighboring countries," said Sourou.

"The politicians and other bloodsuckers have corrupted our sisters, and they've turned to prostitution."

"Have you noticed the condition of this country's roads? The potholes!"

"The minister of public works has called them 'little chickens' nests that give the intellectuals and other anarchistic enemies of democracy a good laugh.' "

"Take a good look at Shoka! Not the residential areas, but the city proper, where eighty-five percent of its two hundred sixty thousand citizens are crammed together. At sunrise it's one huge stench because of the heaps of refuse that pile up daily beside the houses or in the middle of the streets furrowed with cracks."

"Nguvu was also concerned with observed facts of this kind," said his bereaved father—in his fifties, of medium height, thin, sad, with graying hair—in a faraway voice.

Poverty had already drained the life out of him when the calamity struck. The gazes of his son's friends, still crushed by the events, shifted toward him.

"Nguvu wrote about the country's problems. Just a few weeks ago, an African newspaper published a story on tribalism and corruption in Alfajiri. The paper didn't give my boy's name, but the 'minister of men with clubs and bludgeons'* said Nguvu had written it. The minister called him in and bawled him out, accusing him of trying to stir up mess and disorder in this country. Nguvu did not let himself be thrown, and since no one had any proof, the minister let him go. But before he was released, the guys with truncheons came and ransacked the house. They overturned the chests, jars, baskets and even got up under the roofs in three of the huts in our compound. They didn't find a thing."

"Nothing?" said a surprised Koovi, a sturdy young man with a head of stone now bandaged like a mummy after the vicious beating the police had given him before he managed to escape.

"Not a thing. Those types can't read. They took my boy's notebooks, leafed through them, and tried shaking money out of them."

Nguvu's mother, as thin as her husband, who had two other wives, had brought out from her dead son's hut two tied-up cardboard boxes which proved to be crammed with notebooks and folders.

"Here are some things they rummaged through. One of the men with truncheons said he would burn them. The other said it wasn't worth it, that the pinhead student could tell everyone in town or write in the reactionary foreign toilet papers that the police had stolen all his parents' money and burned their clothes."

Houssou undid one of the boxes. He and Nguvu had been best friends. They had been called "the Wassai twins," after their native village, because they were born the same day at practically the same moment. Nguvu's father was off to bring the news of his son's birth to his old friend Konoume when he ran into him walking in great haste to tell him about the happy event that had his whole compound rejoicing. The two men seized each other around the waist, shook each other,

---

*minister of the interior

then took turns hoisting each other off the ground. Their loud and hearty laughter rang through the village. They shared their happiness with their friends, and celebrated with them by downing copious quantities of cashew-nut wine and liquors. Tight as goatskin bottles, they had returned home shouting in the deep night that the "twins of Wassai" would be little jokers worthy of all Alfajiri—men!

Houssou looked through three of the notebooks that were covered with notes, even texts that had been written down, scratched out, corrected, and neatly recopied. He came across marked-off passages that together made up the gist of an incriminating article that had appeared in a newspaper in Senegal, elsewhere in Africa, and also in Europe under headlines like "Something Rotten in Alfajiri," "The Institutionalization of Tribalism," and "Bribery and Tribalism in Shoka."

"Are you sure Nguvu was innocent?" he asked his friend's parents.

"How should I know? I've never been in a white people's country, and I can't read," said Aminifu, the dead boy's mother.

"I think my boy was brave and daring enough to expose what he called 'this country's cancer,' but I can't say whether he was the writer in the paper," explained his father, both sad and proud.

"Nobody here can criticize him for telling the people. Is it a crime to call people's attention to how the men in power are destroying this country? Either you're a patriot or complicitous in the abuse."

"It was suspected that Nguvu had written the articles. I would not disapprove of our poor comrade," added Ajuwa, a tall elegant young woman with velvety black eyes. She had lived in London, taken part in militant progressive movements, and found that the political authorities in Alfajiri practiced Stalinism.

"Me neither," said Houssou, who then read aloud passages marked off in one of the notebooks: "Socially and morally, a terrible gangrene is eating at this country. The authorities themselves are working at it and preventing it from being cut away and brought to light. A few years ago, tribalism was stronger in some parts of the South than in the North. It has become widespread, a spiderweb over the whole country.

"In the North eighty-seven percent of the people interviewed about their reasons for favoring tribalism said that it was 'necessary' because of the persecution we suffered in the South simply because we weren't from the same region or ethnic group.

"In the South sixty-one percent of the people questioned thought that 'the current reaction of our brothers in the North was normal,' and they explained it like this: 'The fault lies with the great tribalists from certain southern tribes, who on getting into power literally stuff the Administration, and diplomatic and party posts, with people from their area or village.

"For the country as a whole, seventy-seven point six percent of those questioned agreed that 'the people whom certain persons appoint because of their tribal loyalties carry on the tribalist politics of their superiors even when these superiors cease being the country's strong men. The administration and the ministerial cabinet are sacred grounds to tribalism in Alfajiri, if we must take the official borders in account.'

"This is a subtle process based on an arithmetic as complex as the Japanese game of go. It is a terrible evil, a cancer becoming institutionalized."

The listeners heaved a sigh, looking as if they had been relieved of a crushing weight.

"Everything Houssou's just read was in that article Nguvu was suspected of writing," said Idoussou, a thin, hearty, intelligent, and extremely restless young man who had escaped the police untouched.

"If the monsters had gotten hold of these notebooks, poor Nguvu would have been arrested and tortured—as the custom now is—and maybe executed to set an example," said Houssou, nicknamed "The Brain" because of his skill in analyzing situations quickly and drawing conclusions or warnings from them.

"Are we going to leave that gang of semiliterate army goof-offs unpunished and all-powerful, while they try and finally succeed in making politics their playground?" asked Kilanko, darting up from his seat.

"We already know you love a fight. But what weapons do you have? What do you suggest we use to combat this race of murderers, who've got rifles and pistols and hand grenades and ammunition?" asked Mewu, "The Philosopher."

"*Shoka!*"*

"*Mashoka! Mashoka elfu moja!*"† said Nguvu's cousin Kungu.

All but two of them burst out laughing. But Noupko suddenly remembered the dance of the venerable Anikokou. As if the idea of a thousand axes had first originated with him, he laid out his plan and described an unusual and well-conceived war strategy. His ideas did not seem spontaneous, and must have matured slowly in his boxy head with its thick, wooly, carefully brushed and parted hair.

"We must even—it is necessary—call on the people to revolt, weapons in hand, against the repression perpetrated by a gang of military power grabbers who've forced this country to live under their bloody dictatorship. Yes, we must stand up and fight, resist aggression and the illegitimacy of a power that tries to silence us and to annihilate the people. Say no to every form of political oppression and dictatorship.

"Haven't you noticed that even insects do not accept the cold ash, but show their opposition by stoutly resisting it and the other decoctions and products our peasant parents use to get rid of them because they attack their crops?

"Are we less than bugs? Are we subinsects that the gang of

---

*a Swahili word meaning "axe." Shoka, the capital of Alfajiri, has the shape of an axe; hence the name.

†a thousand axes (*Mashoka* is the plural of *shoka; elfu* means "thousand"; and *moja* means "one.")

politicians who run this country will end up exterminating?

"Well, children of Alfajiri, we must—as much from necessity as for the dignity of a people rooted in the earth—arm ourselves in unfailing resistance against the oppression, asphyxiation, and death. We are worth more than the insects, and must never be resigned. I have . . ."

"Right! The events of the past weeks prove this. So I think we shouldn't practice the politics of the skeleton in the closet," declared Isdine.

The group, impressed and serious, looked at them as though their ideas had taken them by the throat.

"Brothers, Nguvu was murdered. Comrades were run down by the vans of the repressive public order. There were other crimes. Many comrades are still suffering oppression and torture from the cops and military men who govern us. The situation is clear. We must react, and quickly. If we don't, it will soon be our turn to be caught in their vise and bumped off. So we must act, scour the countryside, quietly find partisans, explain problems to them and convince them of the need for this revolutionary action. Then we should attack without pity the minute we're sure of not being annihilated on the first attempt on the antidemocratic, fascist, and repressive power," said Kungu with an icy calm that gave a few comrades gooseflesh.

But as in a collective dream, they all turned to drill down to the bedrock of the broadly outlined action, by storming the chimeras loaded on the ship of state.

For five months they went through villages and farms, joining with the peasants in their activities. In the evenings, they listened to their hosts tell stories and legends or swap riddles. The students discovered they could use the past to make discreet criticisms of the present, and of the current regime.

"Today we have transistor radios. Every house is required to have one, but it takes three days of work to afford a battery that'll make it run for two or three weeks."

"Yes, if we only used batteries to hear the news that interests us, our plantations and our families!"

"Well said, Zintin! Those guys do a lot of chattering but don't say much, and we don't learn anything."

"Yeah, the president said we must do this and the president said we must do that, and we must pay taxes."

"And taxes, all the time taxes for these ghost people."

"You've got it, Hangnan. How come the president or the minister never comes to see us?"

"Well, they have no need of us, that's it. Since they send guys who take our money, our game, and poultry."

"And when we say no, just a little, they're shoutin' we don't respect the president of the state, and then they hit us with clubs."

"They say the big sin is us peasants 'cast a slur on the dignity of the chief of state.' "

"Who is it who talks to you this way?" asked Koovi, one evening after a hard day's work in the fields, as he was chatting with some of his mother's relatives with whom he liked to come spend the weekend.

"Guys from the party, of course, whadja expect?"

"And the only way—and even that's not certain—to keep them from screaming we're insulting the dignity of the president is to give sheep, chickens, pigs already butchered, and corn and baskets of fruit."

"That can't be true! Aren't you exaggerating a little?" said Koovi.

"What do you mean it's not true? You asking a question or you surprised? Go see the Grandjegbe family, the Azehoutos, the Koudjegans and Bale Anikokou . . ."

"They were victims of the party people?"

"Yeah, they were robbed by the Government guys. The guys from the party."

"And if they tried to stand up to those guys, who are protected by the chief of state, they'd be rotting in jail for a long time."

"And you? Have you been strong-armed, here at this farm?"

"Several times, yes. You know, they come with two or three little trucks and a government car."

"That was their story. To show they were not on a secret mission."

"But us peasants, we let them have an easy time getting our things. We hear their machines coming, we disappear in the bush."

Hessou, Noupko, Awa, Koussie, and other comrades had heard much the same stories and complaints in the villages or farms where they were working. Twice in less than a month they had had to rush for the bush with their peasant relatives who alerted them.

"In reprisal, these representatives of the 'public authority' set fire to a granary at the farm where I work," said Awa.

"They burned down old Anikokou's hut after they beat the poor old man."

"Ah, beating up an old man? That's unheard of!"

"Burning down his house was a crime, but whipping the old man with a blackjack was abusing the very thing Africa reveres most."

"And why? Why'd they do it?"

"When the alarm was given that the militia were on their way, the whole compound cleared out, but old Anikokou refused to come with us. 'I've had enough of running away like a thief because of those snotnosed kids!' and he pulled the sash of his *adire* shorts tight and sat down in front of his house."

"According to what he told us later, the 'snotnoses' asked him questions, shouting at him, asking where were the other people from the compound. They came in the hut, found a dozen axes and hatchets there, and demanded the old man give them the names of the maker and the seller and where he had bought the tools and why. Old Anikokou kept silent in response to so many questions. Then they beat him! And he cried. And he burst out sobbing when he told us."

"Oh, it's not possible!"

"Oh, yes, that's how it was, and it can't go on anymore!" said Noupko, choking with sobs.

"The world is breaking down. The hoods of the revolutionary militia beat an old man who wept but didn't give away any secrets. He betrayed no one. Then, exasperated by this resistance, one of them picked up some straw, made it into a torch which he lit and threw onto the thatched roof of the hut. After committing this crime, the representatives of the 'national authority' left in a hurry. When we came back to the village, the old man told us everything, and two days after that he dies of his troubles, and of his pains, too."

It was a milkily moonlit evening at the foot of the giant oleander that shaded the central court of old Anikokou's compound. The senior maker of edge tools loved these young people who, claiming to have had their fill of the city's annoyances and rot, wanted to remake contact with the soil and the realities of the peasant world. He told them the history of the country which was fertile in wars and alliances between tribes.

"A hundred times the people fell out with each other, a hundred times they made it up, got back together to fight off the foreign invader. They cinched their belts like brave men to resist the aggression of the whites. But after the whites fooled, bought, and corrupted some money-hungry compatriots determined to place their own well-being above the dignity and good of the people of Alfajiri, the whites managed to catch the people in their nets. And so we lost both our dignity and our soul."

Anikokou had sketched for them a people's army made up of peasants, each armed with a hatchet, a club, and a knife. He had told them about the organization and operational strategy of this unusual weapon which haunted everyone's dreams for a week.

The old fighter had also taught his nephew Noupko how to wield the hatchet and the club. Noupko in turn taught Abba, Dossou, Koovi, Essou, Isdine, and Nguki, who were entrusted with the job of collecting the hatchets made by the senior blacksmith and other craftsmen from the outskirts of Kugloxa.

They formed a group called Democratic Forces. They put on peasant clothes, and went to the city, where they sold the axes and hatchets to "comrades with an out-and-out determination to overthrow the repressive order" that ruled Alfajiri.

So, every Tuesday, on market day in Shoka, the new axe vendors left Ilé-Imo and Kugloxa around two in the morning, went some thirty miles with other peasants, and reached the capital around seven. On the way they listened to the conversations of peasants.

"The more we work, the less we earn, but they're yelling every day over the radio that life is getting easier and more interesting."

"Yeah? Interesting for who? For those shiftless good-for-nothings who govern this country."

"If you call that governing."

"It's true, guys coming and making off with our crops and chickens, even money. More like bandits."

"Real bandits do it by night, scared of being caught and beat up and taken off to the police."

"That's true, while the new bandits don't hide their faces. They're well dressed like the whites. They come in cars, threaten, complain, demand, and take everything."

"And if you stand up to them, they whip you like you was a stubborn mule."

"You hear what they did over at Guidiglo's?"

"Seems they whipped him and raped his youngest wife before they took him off to jail, saying he'd insulted the president and spit on the revolution."

"That makes a lot of times the militia guys done that kind of stuff. There's not a day goes by when they don't rape some peasant's wife or daughter and then make him pay."

"And the president and the ministers, there they are in their palace. They don't say a thing to protect us."

"How they gonna protect us poor peasants since the militia guys say they're acting under orders!"

"Yeah, that could be why the president and the ministers criticize the peasants and the shopkeepers, raise taxes, and they say they want to make them even heavier."

"By all the gods, where do they expect us to find the money?"

"Nothing, nothing goes right anymore."

"If that's their revolution, we maybe have to react against it."

"React against it? Are you crazy? Don't you see they've got guns and a lot of the whites' military equipment. Plus, the whites are on their side."

"Yeah, they play the whites' game. They say they're getting rid of the whites' evil in this country, that's true, but they're becoming devils, too."

"So, the peasants should rise up?"

"What you haven't understood is the warning they gave when they jailed Ganglo."

"What'd he do, old Ganglo?" asked Dossa, who two months earlier had heard vague rumors about the village chief of Xwégniko.

"The militia guys and then truncheon men had ransomed and beaten some men of Xwégniko. They even raped the wives and daughters of many peasants. A lot of heads got knocked. Chief Ganglo threatened to complain to the president. 'What? You're going to complain to the president? You're insulting us, you call us thieves. You even raised a hand against us and insulted the austerity of the state. It is the head of the state himself who you have insulted and beaten in our person,' said the militia.

"The truncheon men spouted the same nonsense. Ganglo protested: he hadn't insulted or beaten anyone. He'd protested because his protégés had been abused, mistreated, savagely violated. Well! He went to Shoka. Some say he saw the president. But others say he was beaten, raped, and thrown in prison. True or not, the president named a twenty-five-year-old as the chief of Xwégniko. They say he's the president's nephew and one of the heads of the militia."

At the market the "antirevolutionary nihilists"—one of the expressions used by the government for the rebellious students—knew where to find their comrades who had discreetly become members of the resistance. They came to talk and exchange information with them. They each bought one, two, and sometimes three axes or hatchets, paying handsomely. The parents of several of them had taken the young people's side after the bloody repression in which young men and two girls who weren't students died.

The "antirevolutionary nihilists" had set themselves four months to persuade families to assist in their struggle against a "regime of extortioners, bribers, and murderers." They had partially explained their ideas without revealing their plan.

"Each of you keep at home an axe or hatchet, a sturdy wooden club, and a knife. If they go for us again, we'll hit back. You can impress them by grabbing your weapons. And if they attack you or us too hard . . ."

The warnings and suggestions were first thought of as jokes, but the too-often repeated misconduct of the agents of the government, the militia, and the police persuaded the peasants, workers, and the unemployed to side with the "antirevolutionary nihilists."

Wlanvie, Abiodun, Utamu, and their friends, whom the agents had hunted down, arrested, roughed up, and raped before beating them in the courtyard of the presidential palace, had been released after two months' detention, probably because of the broadsides found in the streets, on the walls and trees, and also because of sharp, often vitriolic criticisms of the foreign press, which had been informed by the official journalists of the revolutionary government of Alfajiri.

The newly "pardoned ones" quickly sized up the situation. They heard about the "governing class" of the "power clique that is unaware of the people's needs."

" 'Once those people got into power,' as my uncle said who

was still in the civil service, 'they became slackers. Born of the people, they no longer know what the people mean or they just have contempt for them. Now it is the people who permanently confront the realities of daily life.'

"And it was a public official who talked that way to his nephew!" said Mewu contentedly.

"The dissatisfaction has affected a small circle in the administration and is even creeping into the National Workers' Union of Alfajiri. But better to keep that whole world in the dark about our activities," said Tunji.

"Thanks to your information, Mewu, Wengi, and I have contacted a few workers. They are discreet, and they don't like either Tonoudouto or the military men in his government whom they lump together as cops. They can handle axes, hatchets, and clubs, and they're ready to help at any time, although they don't know what we're getting them into," said Noupko.

"Isn't that strangely naive and unserious?" asked Tafadheli.

"Probably, so we must be very cautious. If the least suspicion, the least hint gets out about our plan, we'll be feeding these supporters into a grinder that'll shred them to pieces!" said Almohade.

"I hope things don't get to that point," said Wlanvie, whose electrician cousin at the Alfajiri Central Hydraulic Plant had proved to be a determined adherent in the struggle without pity against those in power.

"Rest assured, we'll make every effort not to turn into criminals like the people we're fighting," said Kissegu.

"I'm not trying to set a trap for our young worker comrades, all the less since all of them call the National Workers' Union the 'phalangist army in the service of the government,' and they're right. The one union in Alfajiri barely supports the workers' demands and contributes systematically to the failure of all strikes," said Almohade, with Wengi and Tafadheli's approval.

"The leaders of the N.W.U.A. get something out of the military's stranglehold on this country," said Abiodun.

"Let's not be writing history, it doesn't do any good. The reality right here under our noses and the one that is forcing us to act is due less to the fact that the military grabbed power than to the effects of the exercise of this power, which is a neoimperialist oppression of the people. And it is against this that we must engage in open conflict for which we must now be tightening the screws," vehemently declared Kungu.

After three months of a sporadic strike of classes which the students put to use equipping themselves and setting up ideologically sound operational groups in the countryside within thirty miles of Shoka, the "antirevolutionary nihilists" began regularly attending the high schools, technical schools, and the university. Still, every weekend saw them back on the farms where they continued their training, going many miles on foot through the bush at a charging pace, handling axes, hatchets, clubs, knives, like trained mercenaries brought to bear against the palace guards in Shoka. But they were not mercenaries: children of the country, they defined themselves as a "democratic and popular force" determined to "torment the chimeras that cling to power."

The return of Noupko and his comrades to the university once again provoked some unrest. Law students refused to attend classes, and there was a boycott of political economy and sociology. The next day, the professors of cell physiology and endocrinology again found themselves alone in rooms where students had given them a warm reception at the start of classes. The high schools followed the same tactics. It became impossible to discuss the strike objectively without skirting the ridiculous, but not a day went by without students from three or four university disciplines or high-school or technical-college students staying away from classes or leaving them as soon as they had greeted their teachers.

Without daring to condemn anyone openly, the radio and *The National Awakening* spoke of "bunches of apprentice troublemakers in the University and the educational establishments."

All day long, both these organs praised "the cooperation between the government and the whole country, who were working hand in hand to get ready for the national holiday which our supreme guide General Tonoudouto is determined to make extraordinarily brilliant so as to confirm forever the unity of the children of Alfajiri."

The "supreme guide" added his two cents by getting straight to the point; once again he rounded on the students, calling them "impotents," "legless cripples," and "fake revolutionaries who aren't even funny, for nobody in Alfajiri is amused."

For three weeks, late into the night, neighborhoods all over the city, like villages all over the country, resounded with the beat of the tom-tom, the sound of gongs, and many other instruments. The various ethnic groups or simple social groups practiced, and the preparations for the national holiday progressed, absorbing bureaucrats, workers, and peasants on their way to their families at the end of the workday in Shoka, Lehoue, Tche, Aku, Iku, Obo, Idi, Dhitanji, Watazame, Kuwenda.

For their part, the "antirevolutionary nihilists" sharpened their hatchets and knives at the farms where they were holed up. They drew the iron over the granite blocks they used for grinding, and now and then in the night were heard little dry and peaceful noises of iron blades being filed on pieces of stone.

From time to time, one of them would test the cutting edge with his or her thumb. When the iron broke the skin cleanly as a razor blade or a piece of broken bottle, he or she would stop grinding. Then he would smear a bit of karite-nut butter on the hatchet blade before wrapping it in banana or manioc leaves.

A thousand replicas of this old-fashioned weapon were prepared this way in anticipation of a hypothetical attack.

In Shoka, the municipal authorities, helped by sections of the militia, had loudspeakers set up along the busiest thoroughfares, on the public square, and at every street corner where people instinctively gathered in normal times for distraction or serious talk.

The streets were decorated with streamers in the national colors, paper festoons, multicolored electric lights, some of them—representing fauns, monsters, heads of birds, or ritual masks—connected with blinkers controlled from the National Central Hydraulics Plant.

There were to be public dances and carnivals. The traditional folklore association would give free rein to their talents. And the whole country, animated by a huge breath coming from the heart of the country, would dance until they were out of breath, to the rhythmic sounds of tom-toms, gongs, kpetes, filimbi, assans, and tobas accompanied by songs.

The pace accelerated. In two days, the country would be celebrating. Gathered in Anikokou's old compound, the "anti-revolutionary nihilists" had put their heads together and agreed on their final ideas before setting out for Shoka shortly before sunset. They went through thickets and wooded areas, and into a eucalyptus woods where they enjoyed themselves like children at play. Night came on, and they pitched camp around a bonfire and listened to the evening radio from a small transistor set Almohade always carried with him. Following the general news were details about the preparations for the national holiday, and the political survey of clichés, redundancies, and tedious platitudes.

"Well, the semantic extravaganzas of our national ectoplasm were not programmed," said Khalfani, one of Nguvu's cousins, a handsome, sturdily built man with a cold expression, whose knife and hatchet thrusts were unusually well placed.

"Maybe they're tired," murmured Xwasou.

"Tired or not, there is in Shoka a huge dump run by an agglutination of shits produced during the independence. The state's repressive apparatus must be derailed by attacking it in its gearboxes," declared Maulidi, another of Nguvu's cousins.

They spent the moonless dark night around the fire, and were on the way around four o'clock. The nocturnal dew had moistened the grass, and they caught water droplets from the broad Jerusalem artichoke leaves, big as elephant ears, using them to wash their faces, rub their bodies with both hands, and rinse their mouths.

They now found themselves in a woods of flowering jacarandas through which they jogged, breathing deeply and expiring noisily through their mouths, their breath in the air like steam escaping from a huge boiler.

The sun's rays filtering down into the woods played with the brightly colored berries and the many multicolored flowers. Passion fruits climbed in the close branches of shrubbery, and birds, awakened with the daybreak, quickened the bush with their varied songs.

It must have been two in the afternoon. The "false revolutionaries" were making a lunch of the rest of their provisions, enjoying the cool succulent pulp of the passion fruit. Spotting some branches still bearing flower buds, Noupko and Wengi came close.

"This is a highly symbolic flower," said Wengi.

"I don't know anything about it, but I admit the passion flower is very pretty."

"The whole tragic end of the Christ story can be read in a flower in full bloom."

"Reminiscing about your Christian education and culture?"

"Probably, but it's striking and strangely meaningful to notice so many ever-present realities in an open flower," said Wengi.

"Please! No metaphysics or anthropomorphism, old thing."

"*Ndiyo Bwana. Asante sana rafiki. Lazima twende sasa. Mimi tayari kutoka,*" said Wengi, picking a passion flower.

"Lord, what beautiful things there are in this country!" he murmured.

"Agreed, dream in the woods. That'll increase your energy tenfold."

"Maybe, but we must realize, Noupko, that the city nearly

cuts us off from the very essence of our country," replied Wengi.

"That's true. Here, as at the farms where I spent my 're-treat,' I have the feeling of getting back in contact with the real Alfajiri," said Isdine, who had come up to them.

"Oh, I'm not condemning people who prefer the city to the country."

"Manichean dualities leave me pretty cold, but infrastructures, the implantation of new industries, the creation of schools, universities, the training of skilled workers, and so on and so forth are just so much bait—huge old suction pumps Shoka uses to swallow our villages and countryside," said Taf-sehli, a young sociologist who did not care for Nguvu's "method of approach."

"Oh, bunk. Let's stop spouting on and on about those people. They run the show, that's a fact, and we are like the frogs that wanted to have a king. So, now we don't know what to do with the Great Frog."

"Okay, it's settled. Let's give up this addiction to settling old accounts."

"You're right. Going on and on about the way things used to be is getting away from present realities and we lose sight of the importance of immediate action. So long as we can't go quickly from reflection to effective action, we are 'over-grown children,' the 'eternally colonized despite their inde-pendence,' " said Khalfani.

They spent their second night in the forest. Time suddenly shrank, and from daybreak, the holiday proclaimed itself in an especially romantic dawn with a mauve sky, as though colored by jacaranda flowers. The "nation's smelly degenerates"—as minister Ku-Chinja termed them—remained in the forest. Some of them went into the city to contact friends and give them final instructions.

In the evening, the presidential palace was swarming with fashionable people. The chief of state inaugurated the festivi-ties by giving an unprecedented reception for the diplomatic corps, representatives of foreign firms, and local notables.

Hence, aside from General Tonoudouto, members of his cor-
rupt government, and high-ranking army officers, the bulk of
the guests were whites.

The military orchestra played the new national anthem during which the entire palace was perfectly still, as though suddenly metamorphosed.

Simultaneously broadcast over the radio, the anthem—written to replace the old one which the military government
accused of "decadent bourgeois ideologism and simpering ro-
manticism"—produced the effect of a tragic vanity over the
whole country, while in the distance was heard—muffled, but
precise and moving as though one would have been crushed
by it—the hammer of hobnailed boots on the ground, advanc-
ing toward the enemy in the person of any citizen rebelling
against the power symbolized by the army and the party.

This background noise sent a giant shiver through the people of Alfajiri, a cold sweat or gooseflesh at the world of the
whites resplendent in evening wear and gathered in the courtyard of the presidential palace, bathed in a soft light filtered
by the leaves of the jacaranda and other trees.

But all the guests applauded, shouting, "Long live the Republic of Alfajiri!"

"Long live President Tonoudouto, father of the nation, and
his revolutionary government!"

"Long live the army and the Party of the National Revolution!"

Much food and drink was consumed. The program called
for dancing till dawn. But the "antirevolutionary nihilists"
had already made a discreet entrance into Shoka, contacted
all the comrades posted here and there at strategic points in
the town. They formed a syntagma of the army of earlier times,
of which old Anikokou had given them a detailed description.

At two thirty-five A.M. Lieutenant Colonel Ku-Chinja, minister of the interior, was struck on the brow with a hatchet,
opening up his skull. He gave a great shout, which no one
heard in the swarming gala crowd in the palace courtyard.

He was a tall muscular man with a hard head. He had been

a nurse in Itcha before he was drafted into the colonial infantry and sent off to join the army of Chad, thus involving him in the Second World War. There he had been assistant stretcher bearer and had ended up with the rank of sergeant with two medals for bravery.

Ku-Chinja was bored stiff working at the Royal Ashanti's Hospital when the war in Indochina broke out. He enlisted in a mercenary spirit, killed underdeveloped people like himself, and earned a stripe and other medals for bravery. But history proceeded at the racing pace of a superior athlete. Alfajiri became an independent country, and like many low-ranking military men, he went up through the ranks with a haste that worried his former superiors in the European army.

General Tonoudouto made Ku-Chinja the chief perpetrator of repressions, oppressions, and other harsh measures. The general never denied the police bludgeonings or crimes which his protégé had carried out or covered up.

Three sentries at the palace gates, alerted by Ku-Chinja's cries of distress, gave a start and tried to respond. They trained their submachine guns on the attacker whom they supposed under cover, but they didn't know where. Hatchets came flying out of the dark, whistling though the softly lit air, and decapitated them.

Another sentry went running toward the guests crying, "Revolution! Revolution!"

A hatchet struck him in the back, the iron sunk into his spine as though caught in a steel trap. He still managed to get to the center of the panic-stricken celebrants. One of the president's bodyguards finished him off with a pistol without even looking to see whom he was shooting.

Suddenly, the electricity went off and the whole palace was engulfed in total darkness. There was an inextricable stampede of guests screaming and begging to be spared. The president's well-tested electrical generator was supposed to start up automatically when the area's power went out. But that night the generator did not go on. The military specialist in charge

of illuminating the palace had been killed a half hour earlier
by his assistant, a civilian long won over to the cause of the
"nihilists." When some unknown comrade at the National
Central Hydraulic Plant cut the wires and cables leading to
the palace, soldiers' barracks, and police headquarters, he
scaled the surrounding wall.

"Light! Light, right now!" shouted the chief of state, jostled
by the crowd.

He tottered, fell, and was trampled in the mêlée of terror-
stricken, disoriented guests.

After cracking the skulls of some thirty sentries armed with
submachine guns, the "nihilists" surrounding the palace
clambered over the the wall and invaded the presidential
"paradise." Some were holding torches made of a special hard
resin cut into clubs about three feet long; others were armed
with axes, hatchets, cudgels, and knives hanging from their
belts. They confronted the members of the government and
overcame them. The bodyguards assigned to each of these
distinguished personages reacted against the invaders with sporadic gunfire, killing three of the "antirevolutionary nihilists."

Tonoudouto got to his feet. His members and head had
been trampled in the confusion; he felt a burning sensation
spread over his entire body. In places he felt as though he had
been branded with a red-hot iron, and he was squealing like a
stuck pig. Nevertheless, he made a supreme effort, clutched
his pistol, which he always had on him, even at social recep-
tions. He saw coming toward him axe-wielders who looked to
him like glowing ghosts, invulnerable and fire-shaped monsters
swirling about in a furnace. Tonoudouto squeezed the trigger
and in a final burst of energy shot at one of the ghosts. He
missed him.

Three young men seized him, wanting to take him alive.
But the soldiers, and even some civilians, tried to interfere.
Then the common hatred binding the "nihilist" resisters aimed
true: each axe or hatchet took off the head it infallibly struck.

"Undress!" ordered Maulidi.

Trembling all over, the generalissimo complied.

"Take it all off," said Noupko, imperiously.

The generalissimo looked at him stupefied, the imbecility of his whole person showing on his face like a mask returning from the depths of the ages. He seemed not to understand what he was expected to do or how to go about stripping naked before the "urchins." Almohade and Xwasou appeared. One of them slapped Tonoudouto, the other spit in his face and told him to take off his shorts immediately.

The generalissimo fell on his knees. They got him back up and he carried out the order. Then he appeared naked as the day he was born, but ugly, with a shrunken sex and his bulging testicles hanging like a boxer's gloved fist.

"Forgive me," he murmured.

"What? You're asking forgiveness?" asked the surprised Maulidi.

"Coward! You're pathetic!"

"That's enough. Enough talk," rose the voice of Kungu, dry and uncharacteristically brutal.

The little circle had not finished breaking up when an axe whistled past their ears and took off Generalissimo Tonoudouto's head, which ricocheted against the surrounding palace wall with a sinister thud.

This was Khalfani's doing. The headless body walked straight ahead, with extraordinary dignity, as though it knew where it was going, turned around and made a faultless military salute before collapsing and spilling more blood.

The broadcasting center was occupied. Four of the five guards had been killed at the building's entrance, but the fifth man, who had only had his ear sliced off by a hatchet, surrendered his weapons and immediately put himself at the service of the revolution, declaring he hated the chief of state and the minister of the army. He was, however, taken to the director's office, where he was decapitated at the same time as the director, who had never shown the slightest sympathy for "the young protesters who are doing everything in their power to infiltrate this country with the virus of the depraved, immoral, capitalistic world."

All the radio journalists, except for three technicians who were partisans in the fight against the militia, the party, and the government, fled at the arrival of Hessou, Wlanvie, and Viassin, a lanky, muscular young man with a stern look, who seized the microphone and described the situation.

Connected with the radio station by walkie-talkies, the informants of the "Partisans of Liberation" announced, "Mahoro Tonoudouto cannot do any more harm. His regime has just evaporated."

Viassin announced the news over the air, and went on, "Shoka is in a state of siege. It is urgently requested that all foreigners present in the city and in all of Alfajiri, for whatever purpose, not get involved with what is happening.

"This is an internal matter, a business of the blacks, a settling of accounts between the children of the country.

"Any foreigner, white or black, caught in the act of aiding those in whom the state has ossified will be ruthlessly decapitated.

"No foreigners will suffer from the uprising of this celebration of the national holiday. No harm will come to any child of Alfajiri if he stays home, concerned to enjoy himself in his neighborhood, village, and friends.

"The whites invited to the presidential palace are to leave their vehicles where they are. They are to walk home on foot, their arms crossed above their heads. Any person found in any other position will be executed without trial. Our eyes are everywhere. Our axes, hatchets, and clubs are following every person. Every suspicious gesture vis-à-vis the Thousand Axes will be fatal to the person who makes it.

"The revolt is making its flowers of blood bloom. The officers' camp is surrounded. The central prison is empty. It contained more victims of despotism than genuine criminals.

"Ku-Chinja, the minister of the interior, is dead. His body lies inert in the palace courtyard.

"Second Lieutenant Mahoro Tonoudouto, head fascist who promoted himself to generalissimo and chief of state, has just died.

"The presidential palace, surrounded by the Thousand Axes rebels, will be bloodied and set on fire if the fat guests invited by General Tonoudouto make a false move, the slightest act of reaction against us.

"The Thousand Axes are determined to purify the country of an illegal power ruling by despotism, dictatorship, oppression, and enslavement of the peasants and poor people for the benefit of some feudal landowners and imperialist weeds.

"Peasants and young people who have helped us, take your axes, hatchets, clubs, and overcome the militia who mistreat you.

"And you comrades positioned near or under the very roof of certain big shots or representatives of the army or police, you already have axe and club within reach. Be on the alert. Act without pity against anyone favoring Tonoudouto's ectoplasmic government, but let the celebration continue.

"Let the people enjoy themselves. It is in its name and in its interest that the children of Alfajiri are rising up against the neoimperialism we must destroy, even if we ourselves have to die.

"Long live the republic!

"Long live democracy!

"Long live freedom!"

As the news traveled throughout the capital and the rest of the country, the people, as though a crushing weight had been lifted off their backs, cheered wildly and went back to their dances in the festival halls: the holiday went on. The antirevolutionary nihilists were amazed by this. The torch carriers invaded the palace courtyard. The flames from the resinous clubs of the "fighting torchbearers" moved about all over the presidential palace, looking like ghosts. They stepped over corpses, walked on the dying bodies that the armed partisans would abandon to their fate or finish off with a club or axe blow in the case of a member of the government or some particularly unpopular personage.

They made their way all over the palace, checking offices

and apartments. No looting took place. They did not destroy a single document from the archives, or even break a plate. A noise caught Utamu's attention; it was as if a light breath were playing with the crystals of a chandelier. He made a sign to Gitonga and Houinsou, two peasants from the three hundred and thirty who had arrived in the capital the night before the national holiday because he had told them to be there just in case . . .

The three partisans, hatchets ready, advanced toward the spot where Utamu had heard the tinkling. There they saw Idowu Ologbo, the minister of education, at the end of a rope attached to the bolt from which was suspended the huge bronze chandelier of the ministers' conference room. For a fraction of a second, their ears rang with prolonged cheers and laughter of the gargoyles, fauns, and obscene characters sculpted or pyrographed by the country's artisans on the frieze at the ceiling.

"Coward! He chose suicide rather than face the consequences of a revolt that he had helped to cause."

Special sections had been assigned to get a viselike hold on the municipal and national police. The watchword was steely hardheartedness toward those identified as unsympathetic to young people. It was agreed that the life of any wife or child of the besieged ones would be spared unless they raised a hand against a partisan, in which case they would be mercilessly exterminated. They had to separate the wheat from the chaff, and at the gendarmerie and police station the partisans ordered the men to cross their arms over their heads and to proceed single file to the ballroom.

Once there, they were told to get completely undressed and again to raise their arms above their heads. They complied without a murmur of protest. The partisans recognized and promptly killed some representatives of the government's repressive organization.

Wlanvie burst in with five comrades. Like all the other nihilists she had her face caked with kaolin and her eyes ringed with *udongo mwekundu*, the simple disguise making them all look like monsters. Spotting Corporal Ubaya and his superior Mende, she took one step up to Ubaya. His flaccid sex retracted still further, looking like the tiny snout of a rat hesitating to come out of its hole. Wlanvie took the organ between her thumb and index finger and pulled it toward her. The man tried to react, but saw two hatchets raised against him. With a quick gesture, without saying a word, Wlanvie drew her knife from her side and chopped off Ubaya's penis and testicles.

The man gave a great cry, fell on his knees, doubled up, then crumbled in a pool of blood. Wlanvie headed for Mende, who charged on her. A hatchet blade planted itself in the back of his head. He turned around, his back covered with blood, facing Wlanvie. Her still-bloody knife stabbed him in the abdomen.

"Forgive me! Oh, forgive me!" he cried as he collapsed.

Wlanvie recovered her weapon. She rejected Mende's plea with a kick in the face, and he fell back. She took his penis and cut it off, too. The sergeant gave a final cry which reverberated throughout the barracks. It was the voice of a man accustomed to command and who liked to make himself heard at some distance.

"The barracks has been purged of thirty bludgeon wielders unworthy of our country. We hope this will be a lesson for you who will be called to defend democracy," said one of the partisans.

"At the police station, all known killers were exterminated," said Koovi.

"Stay where you are, and don't move until you are given the authorization. The eyes of the partisans everywhere are trained on you and observe your gestures. One false move and the barracks will go up in flames, and you and your families, to whom the democracy grants a reprieve, will be burned to death," declared Hessou in a steady, cold, persuasive voice.

The group got back to the presidential palace, while Dansou—torch in one hand, hatchet in the other—went on guard in front of the barracks with its high walls studded with pieces of broken bottles. He was a strapping young man with intelligent eyes, an edge-tool maker from Xoxa, a village some thirty-five miles from Shoka. His present mission was to set fire to the barracks if a single gendarme tried to escape.

The walls of the gendarmes' garrison, like the walls of the army camp, had been wetted down with gasoline. The evening before, young firemen very quickly converted to the "nihilist" cause had made some large barrels available to the insurrectionists. Going into action when a current was cut at strategic points agreed on by the armed young people, the firemen had hosed the walls with gasoline. One spark and it would be hell. Dansou had been forewarned and kept at a respectful distance, while watching this "house of hate" where the enclosed women and children screamed in anguish.

Three in the morning. On concluding their operation in the palace and after they had inspected the offices and living quarters, the partisans went back to the courtyard. The guests were still there, some standing, others sitting down, but all with their arms crossed over their heads.

One European talked of bloody anarchists and murderers.

Abiodun was passing nearby at just that moment, and suddenly her hatchet broke open his skull, and the distinguished man's white flannel dinner jacket was soaked in blood.

"Why? Why did you have to say that, Georges?" screamed the victim's wife, who threw herself on the body.

"You heard us, Madame. This business is between blacks, between the children of Alfajiri. Any white person, any foreigner who gets mixed up in it will be ruthlessly decapitated," said Abiodun, now joined by some comrades.

The night turned into tender reddish daylight, like a distant dying brushfire. From the radio station rose the pure, calm voice of Kungu.

> *Je! Wananchi ya Alfajiri! . . .*
> *Tafadhalini sikiliza habari!*
> *Ndiyo . . . Tumeshinda adui vitani,*
> *Na tushangilia sana!*

Sasa mwangaz alfariri na mapema juu ya Alfajiri
Na hasa hapo ndipo mi jacaranda
Huonyesha miurujuani yake! . . .

Citizens of Alfajiri,
Please listen to the news!
Yes, we've bested the foe in the struggle
and demonstrate our triumph!
Now on Alfajiri begins glistening
a dawn new and tender
and already the jacarandas truly offer us
their mauve sweetness!

"Citizens of Alfajiri, one foreigner has been executed for calling members of the liberation movement bloody anarchists and murderers. We trust this act will serve as a lesson to foreigners who have come to our country to get rich and have always supported the torturers' stranglehold on our country's wealth, culture, information, and education.

"The time is three fifteen. In three-quarters of an hour, all the whites located here in the palace of the republic and who are afraid to go home on foot will have returned to their domiciles.

"The soldiers, gendarmes, policemen who have been spared are commanded to go to Republic Square with the army and highway department trucks, collect the bodies, and go burn them at a pyre ready for them at Mintaklo.

"Not one body will be buried.

"The eyes of the Thousand Axes are everywhere and will see anyone who resists.

"Every theater of insurrection of this past night must be cleaned and disinfected by the army, the police, and the gendarmerie with the cooperation of the highway department, under the surveillance of the National Sanitation Service.

"The Constitution, which was never respected and was systematically violated, is hereby dissolved.

"The party is abolished.

"All the representatives of the party militia have been suppressed, and the word 'militia' is stricken from our country's vocabulary.

"Power is solemnly declared vacant.

"The vacuum so created will last until the election, with universal suffrage, of a president worthy of Alfajiri.

"No military figure will ever again govern Alfajiri.

"The civilians, old political campaigners, were imprisoned by the fascist military regime. The Thousand Axes have freed them.

"These hidebound old alligators are formally requested to keep out of it. No person older than forty may be a candidate for the presidency of the republic, and there will be no more than five candidates.

"The new day dawning is declared a holiday. The people must recover from the past night's anguish.

"Children of Alfajiri, in a few hours you will see no more axes or hatchets or clubs in anyone's hand. But the Thousand Axes to be buried in the breaking dawn are everywhere. They are in the tender gaze of a wife looking at her husband, of a husband looking at his wife, in the smile of your children, in the embrace of our brothers or your friends, under the table in our office, in the soil we cultivate, ready to loom forth if the slightest attempt is again made on democracy and the republic.

"Any misuse of power will be punished.

"Any rape, theft, or misappropriation will be punished with the axe.

"We are entering a new era and it is requested of both students and pupils, as we ourselves are, to resume attending classes which teachers and professors will conduct democratically.

"All production must be resumed. Any dereliction will be punishable by death.

"Long live the republic!"

Everything happened the way the radio had announced. No one, except friends of the late Nguvu, knew who had spoken.

All weapons vanished before five o'clock in the morning. The bodies that had been taken away were loaded onto trucks headed for Mintaklo. As if it were a matter of a quite local news item, nothing prevented the rest of the city, and even less the country, from feasting and dancing.

A few curious people, come to the vicinity of the palace of the republic around seven o'clock, noted that everything was normal there.

"Except the president was wiped out."

"So it seems."

"It was a nice clean piece of work. The guys didn't destroy a thing."

"Yeah, everyone's noticed it."

"So we don't have a president or ministers?"

"Well, for the good they did this country . . ."

"They were pains in the neck. Even the guys my father had known as kids and who were still coming to our place three months before going into politics, even those guys had become arrogant."

"Yeah, bandits who had everything."

"Now we wait and see."

"Nothing will be like it was before."

"You think?"

"Well, the people who call themselves Thousand Axes also say they are everywhere."

"Could you be one of them yourself?"

"And you too, probably?"

They burst out laughing, clapping each other on the back, and then stared at each other in surprise.

Translated from the French by Franklin Philip

EDMOND JABÈS

WITH NELSON MANDELA

🤍

You are near me. Are you free?
I am far from you. Am I free?
Freedom scoffs at time and distance.
And yet, it may only be for a moment
free and, localized, in one conquered region.

These allusions to Nelson Mandela came back to mind from one of my books.

Thoughts about freedom, as though freedom also had to be thought out, these few lines followed by others like this:

Freedom links me to the freedom I have mastered.

or this:

To aspire to freedom is to foster the same aspiration in others. This reversal of bonds is called brotherhood, the bonds no longer constraining, just the leavening of blended freedoms.

The right to freedom is in the end just the right to be a man among men.

And as though this right were acquired for good.

Enclosure is not always closure. It may be infinite opening.

The obstacle to raze is the wall. Mind and heart know sturdier obstacles.

There are walls of smoke.

There are walls familiar to freedom, for without them no man would know he had at least once been free.

Freedom asserts itself every day at every moment.

And what is that voice, stronger than stone riveted to stone, stronger than the prison's iron bars that day slips in between and that night comes to grip?

White hands of dawn, warming the inmate's shadow-streaked hands, grasping the bars of his prison. Black hands of evening, groping in the dark for the same discouraged pair of hands.

The prisoner's clenched fists, like the point of ink at a sentence's end—decisive, but not final. While there remains a word or line to write, there will be no final period.

Our freedom is this word, these sentences, whatever they may be. Live words defying the world and lighting the universe with a light intense enough to blind or dazzle, to wound or amaze enough to force our eyes to close. The most inward of all lights.

Mandela, by the name of almond, sweet to one who knows its savor, bitter to one who knows its bitterness.

This name is synonymous with freedom.

This name is the fruit of the dew-covered almond tree in the morning, soaked with salubrious rain or hundreds of thousands of tears.

O, people that has its tree. Its generous unshakable witness; dancing plant mobile amid its dances; singing soul of the joyful earth amid its songs, but shivering, trembling with the child, the woman, the fighter, who revere it, frustrated inhabitants of a conquered country, the one where, with them, it grew up.

Trembling for every second of life of a population left to itself; trusting, however, like it, in the future; in the future's many and promising cuttings, which are also its roots.

▲ ▲

Today, the hands that planted this tree reach, open, for its branches, not waiting for the comfort of a word, the precious gift of a fruit, but in their shadow, are saturated with their silence. Thus, emptied of their content, our futile words are rotting within a word returned to its mute eternity.

These stubborn hands are the conscience of a people fashioned, sculpted by silence. Its lone chance to survive.

Ah, do not let them one day curl round a dagger's handle. Let them not renounce caresses, having opted for revenge.

One cannot count on the word when stagnating in a prison cell. It risks being a mere auditory display of naught.

The word blooms in public.

But silence? Who dares take it on?

Alliance. Not to unclench the teeth. Cut short the word. Keep secret. Keep. Keep.
Silence is the total rejection of ineligible words—not negation, but disqualification.

Silence is truth. This truth lives in the recorded word of a people. Makes its hunger for freedom hungrier. Makes its thirst for justice thirstier.
Dreamer, thinker, hero, martyr, Mandela embodies this silence, personifies this tree. Hence he is invincible.
How could his tormentors stamp out a man whose silence already reduces them to nothing?

Translated from the French by Franklin Philip

HEINER MÜLLER

WOYZECK—THE WOUND

▼

1

As Woyzeck continues to shave his captain, to eat the prescribed peas, to torment Marie with his dumb, stifling love, his people have become a state, surrounded by specters: the hunter Runge is his bloody brother, proletarian tool of Rosa Luxemburg's assassins; his prison is called Stalingrad, where the murdered victim approaches him in the guise of Kriemhild; her memorial stands on the hill of Mamayev, her German monument, the wall, in Berlin, the armored train of the revolution now congealed to politics. MOUTH PRESSED AGAINST THE SHOULDER OF THE CONSTABLE, WHO NIMBLY LEADS HIM AWAY, Kafka saw him disappear from the stage, after the fratricide SUPPRESSING WITH EFFORT THE LAST WAVE OF NAUSEA. Or as the patient, into whose bed one puts the doctor, the wound gaping like an open mine with worms flicking from it. His first manifestation was Goya's giant who, sitting atop the mountains, counts the hours of domination; father of the guerrilla.

On a mural in a monastery cell in Parma I have seen his severed feet, gigantic in an arcadian landscape. Somewhere his body may be bounding ahead on his hands, perhaps shaking with laughter, into an unknown future, which might be his encounter with the machine, propelled against gravity amid the soaring flight of rockets. In Africa he is still doing his Stations of the Cross leading him into history, time is no longer on his side, even his hunger may no longer be a revolutionary element since it can be relieved with bombs, while the tambour-majors of the world ravage the planet, battlefield of tourism, launchpad in the event of disaster, without paying heed to the fiery images the Orderly Franz Johann Christoph Woyzeck saw leaping across the sky near Darmstadt, when he was cutting sticks for the run of the gauntlet. Ulrike Meinhoff, daughter of Prussia and latter-day bride of another foundling of German literature, who killed himself near Lake Wannsee, heroine of the last drama of the bourgeois world, the armed RETURN OF THE YOUNG COMRADE FROM THE LIME-PIT, is his sister wearing the bloody necklace of Marie.

2

This text, many a time abused in the theater, happened to a twenty-three-year-old, who had his eyelids cut away by the fates at birth, blasted by fever down to the very orthography, a structure of the kind that might emerge after pouring molten lead into water on New Year's Eve, when the hand holding the spoon trembles before that look into the future, a sleepless angel, it blocks the entrance to paradise, where the innocence of play-writing once made its home. How harmless the meager crop of recent plays, Beckett's WAITING FOR GODOT, before this sudden thunderstorm that arrives with the swiftness of another age, carrying with it Lenz, the extinguished spark from Livonia, the time of Georg Heym in the utopialess space under the ice of the Havel River, of Konrad Bayer in the gutted cranium of Vitus Bering, of Rolf Dieter Brinckmann's right-hand traffic in front of SHAKESPEARE'S PUB; how shameless the lie of the POSTHISTOIRE in the face of the barbaric reality of our prehistory.

3

HEINE THE WOUND begins to scar over, crookedly; WOYZECK is the open wound. Woyzeck lives, where the dog lies buried;

the dog is called Woyzeck.* For his resurrection we wait with the fear and/or hope that the dog will return as a wolf. The wolf comes from the south. When the sun reaches its zenith, he will become one with our shadow and, at the hour of incandescence, will begin history. Not before history has happened will it be worthwhile to share oblivion in the frost of entropy, or politically abbreviated, in the atomic flash, which will be the end of utopias and the beginning of a reality beyond mankind.

Translated from the German by B. M. Linke

---

*Translator's note: The author here expands the image of a German idiomatic phrase: *Da liegt der Hund begraben*—"that's the sore point"—which literally translates as "there the dog lies buried."

SEVERO SARDUY

It goes without saying this is not a poem about Nelson Mandela or present-day South Africa in any specific way. It is, rather, an homage to what black culture and learning have given to my country (Cuba), her music, and universal knowledge. The brief poems that follow sketch a history of jazz, beginning with its African origins and moving to South America, Cuba (where it produced such great artists as Pérez Prado, Benny Moré, etc.), and eventually New Orleans. The poems also contain a brief history of the nightclubs that contributed to the diffusion of this music, as well as allusions to painting (for instance, to the famous boogie-woogie series that Piet Mondrian painted in New York while dancing). Jazz returned to Africa, thus tracing the flight of a boomerang. Its trajectory on the map of the world makes a black spiral. Hence the title of one of the poems.

MOOD INDIGO

let me engrave rattles upon your cheeks
write on your forehead with chalk
paint spiral stripes on your sex
upon your buttocks, fluorescent disks

        white lines of dots
        survey your black body

let me autograph your head
cover your feet with plaster
your hands with gold flowers
Egyptian eyes upon your chest

        white ideograms
        your body a black map

Tantric Band

Cootie Williams on the trumpet-femur.
Joe Nanton on the trombone: to get a good wa-wa
        piss in the brass mouthpiece.

Johnny Hodges on the alto sax: a grand lama, yeah man
        Who else could blow out of his mouth the air
        inhaled up his ass?
Harry Carney on the baritone sax, a grand lama, yeah man.
        Who else could blow out of his ass
        the air inhaled through his mouth?
Sonny Greer on the drums: the timbrels:
        child skulls sawed down the middle
        authentic yak skin.
Duke at the piano in flames.

          with Benny Morton's trombone
          and Dizzy Gillespie's trumpet
          tasted by virtuosos
          in black sweat
drugs
          stowed away on a boat
dancing
          on a steamboat

sophisticated
  new gold fetish
    double arabesques
      engraved with stones and feathers   god
     ivory dice   black notes   given
       a rusting trumpet

                                        antelope
                                        ornaments

                        the Douanier
                        dreams
                        serpent
                        flute
covered with red cuneiforms
striped flash
a passing tiger
murmur of orchids rotting

SUN filtered through a bamboo   fence
  boats rolling—the band on board—: brass
                          shining   SUN

splattered fetish semen blood clots
white stones eyes
in the temple of Ochum
          amber
          by the immobile
          river
          whirling conch shells

                          opal
                          amulets

                    black
            panthers

    shutters sealed
        with planks doors nailed shut
        with sand bags and broken mirrors
        amulets seal the windows

            spells kill whites
                Jean Genet in a forgotten valise

            machine guns
                tear it all down
            Echoes of Harlem striped
                    cyclone
                hash brownies
                    zero
            Nina at the piano
                    raze it all to the ground
                        the next time   fire!

with hoarse rattles
splinters of glass
Cootie Williams at the trumpet
and the Duke at the piano
with wooden claves
they've written in Yoruba
mute dog bites
double drums   with Ray Nance on the violin
wood and leather clepsydras   with Duke at the piano
mark time with the beat of the game   *gold feathers*
the falling ashes of your bones   the ashes of your bones falling

black like milk
like teeth   black
the same black of the baptismal waters

snow

black like the page
of glass fiber   black
cornea of the eyes

semen

with white signs on your cheeks
chalk on your forehead
no salt for the thirst
in your skin and bones

onyx
white tattooed spirals
feather castles on your head
a text on your face
written with plaster
in ebony

Black Spiral

to Piet Mondrian dancing

to the woogie-boogie

to the boogie-woogie

to the Haig

to the Cigale

to the Cotton Club

to Chori's again

to the Tin Angel

to the Riverside

on your ankles

with bells

on your wrists

of the Gold Coast

from the Congo to Virginia

with elegguas

box bone bottle

Antilles bamboo

flasks filled with stones

to New Orleans

to Havana

rattlebones

to Congo Square

from Nigeria to Rio

triangle banjo skins   from the black center   to Saint-Germain

from Rio to Recife   with rattles

from the river   to the Tabou

with cigar boxes   with feather castles   to the Cameleon

to Eddie Condon   with gold bracelets   to the Half Note

to Chori's

to the Central Plaza   the enslaved kings   spiritual/spiral   to the Café Bohemia

tattooed cheeks

immobile like a river   to Nick's

to the Stuyvesant Casino   wasn't dat a wide ribber

to the Society

to Jimmy Ryan's   to the Café Métropole

tiny red arrows

to the Ember's   to Birdland

to the Voyager's room

to the Composers

to the Savoy ballroom   to Carnegie Hall

to the Apollo Theater

to Juilliard School

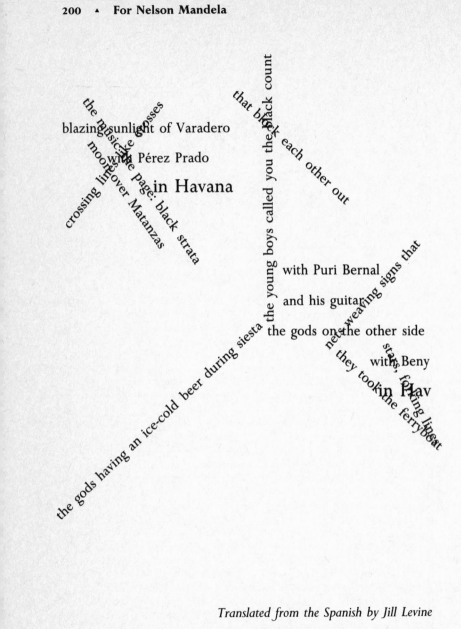

blazing sunlight of Varadero
with Pérez Prado
in Havana

the music like crosses
over the page: black strata
moon over Matanzas
crossing limits

that black count
each other out
the young boys called you the black

with Puri Bernal
and his guitar
the gods on the other side

net weaving signs that
stray, fixing lines

with Beny
in Hav
they took the ferryboat

the gods having an ice-cold beer during siesta

Translated from the Spanish by Jill Levine

HÉLÈNE
CIXOUS

THE PARTING
OF THE CAKE

▼

What I am about to relate is what I began seeing as I closed my eyes to make my imaginary way to South Africa and spoke the name Mandela. At length I suddenly succeeded in drawing near. By way of Mandela. Up to then, each time I tried, my timid, horror-filled imagination went dead.

Apartheid will not stop shamelessly uttering its real name, "apart-hate," with its putrid breath. I long feared that breath as if it issued from the Devil. It is indeed the Devil, making me keep my distance.

I was afraid, and I was afraid until one fine day I smelled the perfume of milky almond finally pierce the filth of apartheid.

It was a perfume of the soul, the strong yet delicate perfume of the great loves, the almond perfume of the Mandelas. The perfume of a love stronger than death. Almandela! A perfume of the triumph of good over evil. How good the Good smells when it has triumphed! A perfume clinging enough to go through seven hells without losing a single magic molecule.

I say "Mandela" and my mouth has the subtle taste of fresh almonds, the taste of the milk of that biblical fruit, hiding its firm sweetness within its hardness.

I have a desire to talk about Winnie and Nelson Mandela—two tall people who for some time have been magnificently striding my thoughts—but it is hard to do, for they are sacred. One cannot talk about the sacred with mere ordinary words, which dry up on leaving the mouth. The sacred must be spoken of with a passion that is shy, as in asking forgiveness. And at the same time the sacred demands weeping and rejoicing.

How dare I talk about such a cruel story, one neither I nor anyone close to me has lived through, one I will never have to suffer.

It will be an honor. I shall therefore proceed without the modesty that so resembles pride.

I shall now make a declaration of love for Nelson and Winnie Mandela.

History was already moving fast that day in 1958 when they met.

And of all the stories in history, theirs moved the fastest.

Though still living, they already are part of the world's memory. They entered it on the twelfth of June, 1964, the day their future began.

What they very nearly haven't had is a present. What is called time: a beginning with an end. They have never had time to complete a moment, an hour, a meal, a conversation. Everything begun has not finished. Everything has been interrupted. But what they have in abundance is absence and its vicissitudes.

"Life with him was, right from the start, life without him." My beloved is the husband of the people. My wife is the mother of the people. "I never had any light-hearted romance. There was never any time for that."

No time for the good little things in life, no time for the bad little things in life. Between them no details, no explanation, no negotiation, no doubt, no wavering between two hesitations. One can parley with God, but no time in the face of Africa.

Only beforehand the infinite acceptance. The running answer before every request. Only a *oui, oui,* the name of Winnie.

But Winnie's real name, her black name, is Zami. In Xhosa Zami means "test."

A single *oui* a single time for every occasion. A *oui* determines their fate. He didn't ask me to marry him. He said, "How many bridesmaids do you want?"

I didn't ask him if he was divorced.

And everything was already understood for good.

Because they lived the passion beforehand and for centuries according to Africa Triumphant.

And the era without time immediately began. Their story has no now. Love without broad daylight, only dawns and twilights.

"At dawn I would be waiting for the sacred moment when he would tap on my windowpane." At dawn the whole world ceased to breathe. Listened. He will tap at the eternal window, he who is coming to her taking the road of every passion.

And all the dawns quiver with sacred possibility.

From 1958 to 1964 each day was the Song of Songs, the song of Nelson and the rose of Bizana, the song of panting early mornings, arise my love, from Orlando, from Pretoria, he is coming, he of the nights full of *venance*, nights damp with the hope of him, nights not sleeping, nights looking for him, nights hearing him come through the mountains, over the hills, between the police nets, and he never stops coming, he arrives, he's only a few centuries, a few miles from my arms, a few moments from my lips, a few walls away, it was the song of moist flesh and bunches of grapes and apples and fig leaves at the barred window, Oh, everything taps at the sacred window, all the fingers that are not yours, the fingers of wind and rain, the fingers of the jacaranda, until finally his fingers tap, his moon voice in the dark, for the winter has just passed, come, it is the time of flowers and doves, the time of places to hide in the stairwell, crevices in the rock of time, "I never knew when," when one never knows what when, each when is called soon, now, always, at any moment he comes, the air fills with his steps, there love pushes the moist door of the night,

the heart of Winnie fights in Orlando, and her body stretches west to Capetown and east to Pietermaritzburg and north to the Limpopo River, walk over me my love, I'll not let you go till you've trampled me with love. The soldier guarding the district found me—they ransacked my house, the drawers, my bed filled with traces of him, oh my soul's love does not come does not tap on the pane, my women friends, my sisters from Bizana by the gazelles and zebras of the veld, I conjure you up, that he doesn't appear, that he looms out of the desert like the tamed lion scented with frankincense and myrrh,

come don't come I call you but you don't answer, I want you to flee but I want you to come, through fire and guns one more time again, for I am ill with need.

The day wild waiting, alarmed, she looks for him in the papers, she doesn't find him in Capetown, she finds him in Pretoria, hallelujah he's alive, her heart scours the nation, she is jealous of every crowd, every village, every friend, I didn't see him yesterday but people in Port Elizabeth did, my beloved is the most beloved of beloveds, but I am the one who loves him most and let it be me he loves the most I desire him and I want him but I cannot demand him, for my love belongs first to his people who love him, he is the husband of all Africa,

but he taps only at one windowpane, at the window of the too-small cottage in Orlando. Never at a window were there so many prayers and so many tears held back and so much desolation, so many death agonies and resurrections.

All this when Nelson was only "accused" of treason and still so divinely possible, no bar around him, merely men and the packs of the Law, and while it could happen that he comes, that he truly arrives one day or another and no matter when.

Scarcely time to fall from love, to love him, with such great difficulty the time to be loved by him, to be loved by her. In fact only the time to begin loving him and right away losing him and desiring her and right away it is time to hope for each other.

"I didn't have time to unlove him. No time to reach the enough, to stay in his house, to forget him a little, to relish him, I never knew peace in my belly, the sleeping silence of the flesh, always this cry this hunger."

"I didn't close my eyes, I wasn't Winnie's baby, her lion cub, her secret son. I didn't slip stretched out in a dream through the sweet fluvial night filled with stars. I stayed awake. I fathered two daughters in two lightning bolts. And I vanished. I could never stop being tall and imposing and Nelson Mandela. If I put down my weapons just one time . . ." All the things he could not do.

All the things she could not do:

hum a distracted tune while making jam
go with him to buy groceries
run errands without him, not giving him a moment's thought,
  like a woman alone some Saturday morning in spring
go out leaving him still in bed in the house, and finding him
  in the house on her return
tell him she wouldn't be back tonight because she was going
  to a meeting of the Women's Federation, for he'd already
  left before sunup with no chance to tell her what meeting
  he was going to
dither some morning between three dresses and ask him which
  she should wear
set the table for him and the children, then see themselves
  truly at table, all four of them
one day refuse to do what he wanted. Once, at least. She
  wanted to say no. And for him to say: good. But that was
  truly impossible. In their life there wasn't a minute to dis-
  agree. Especially as it was pointless to speak up in disagree-
  ment, for they always ended up agreeing.
So, life always had the purity of a skeleton. But this was not
  by choice

ask him why he chose number 8115, the smallest house in
Orlando, a bungalow with only a front room, bedroom, and
kitchen, when he could have picked the four-room place
next door, since in the forties he had the right to do this,
and the chance too, and there was no harm in that. Not
that she doesn't know the answer, but to make him realize
that she, thinking about how the children have to make do,
regrets the choice
make him realize she's not a saint, otherwise what credit
would she get for loving him as she did, and for bearing up
when so much was unbearable
make a scene, which she would need to do more than once,
for a woman living in Africa—even one with the privilege
of being married to such an admirable man—sometimes
finds herself in an unpleasantly ancient situation of which
a man doesn't even suspect the causes or the existence.

Let alone that a woman anywhere needs to make a scene
now and then.
For example, when he would get back from the tribunal
with ten surprise dinner guests when he knows there's only
one chop in the refrigerator and he forgot it, and he's bragging
you'll see what a great cook my wife is, she really couldn't
stand it. But she could never bring herself to tell him. Here
was a man already on trial for treason. And he was the most
just and innocent man in the country.
Innocent he had always been. That's what made life so
athletic.
Because it's much harder to love an innocent person than
one who behaves foolishly.

They never parted, they were torn apart.
Someone came to fetch me in an old pickup, a big guy in
a white dustcoat. When I got in with him, it was He. He
drove the wreck downtown, talking very fast I didn't cry out
with love, I put my hand on my life's knee and drew life into
my body, I lived. In town, at a red light, he told me I'll come

back, stay well, my darling, vanished, at the corner of Sauer Street, I didn't have time to shout I'm dying, this life is killing me, I slipped over to where he'd been sitting, my buttocks in the impression left by his, my hands on his hands, his hands under my hands, I felt his blood go into mine, hundreds of whites crossed the street.

At the wheel of solitude in Johannesburg, my lungs filled with groans, there's no room in my breast for the storm. The truck would likely explode. Howling, in howled name. Oh, to be a dog or a donkey and bray with pain to the clouds! Let loose the cry down to the last croak! Right downtown. Impossible!

She will make a scene one day. Before God.

In March 1961, at the conclusion of the trial for treason, Nelson came to the house accompanied by Sisulu, Nokwe, and Joe Modise.

He was standing in front of the door. "Sweetheart, pack my suitcase. I'll be going away for a long time." Take care and don't worry, friends'll be bringing you news. I know you'll be strong enough to go on without me.

He was standing in front of the door, but I couldn't get to him, so many well-wishers were crowding around.

I quickly packed his suitcase. When I started to take it to him my love wasn't there. He'd gone. I'm leaving for a long, long time. An hour later someone came to pick up the suitcase. When I left, he wasn't there. The leave-taking filled my heart.

The next day I read in the papers that he'd spoken before a huge crowd in Pietermaritzburg. He's talked to his people four hundred miles from my heart. But my heart heard every word.

Kneeling before the tall sacred woman I list the pains. The lack and anguish make her majestic. "I need warmth, I need human bread, I need tender human flesh to nourish my empty arms, I need my share of the cake of life." For a long time she sustained herself lightly with her nursing daughter Zindzi. For it is good for daughter to suckle mother.

It was not easy having a life of destiny and Africa for a family name. For, even so, he was just a man, she just a woman with a desire to cry. They have labored so hard, but unheroically, especially she. With difficulty, with terror, with such pities. But, I believe, being tested and crying out unheroically is what heroism means. And also laughing whenever possible.

Zami and Nelson began to marry in June 1958. It would be a perfect marriage, the marriage of the future. Both traditional and modern, it would unite east and west, heaven and earth, Xhosa kin and Thembu kin, ancestors and descendants, fire and rain, lachrymal salt and salivary sugar, hope and certainty, ostrich and hunter, faith and science, black learning and white learning.

All these vows went into the dough for the marriage cake.

The first half of the cake is to be eaten with the family of the bride, the other half with the family of the groom. When the dough is fully blended with the human dough, the force of the cake of desires begins acting.

Zami and Nelson's cake was uniquely magical:

In Bizana, just as Zami and Nelson began eating the Pondo half of the cake, the telephone rang, they couldn't finish, whisked by a gust of wind to Johannesburg, everything was interrupted, the celebration, the cake, the dough, desires, separated, the reality of the other side, the dance, cut, the cake shouted, the wind blew, the telephone roared, the sentence fell. Happily the separation was not between them, but in them, in the soft part of their flesh. Both felt the pain cutting their bodies and while a dust storm accompanied them back to the city, each nearly wept with pity for the body of the other. In the plane they smiled at each other, their gazes mingled, a cake of the soul was baking. Each with eyes swelling with tenderness mutely showed, I am hungry for you, my love. The two hungers were married.

And the cake? The cake is made of the same dough as their love. It is a cake of superhuman resistance. It had all their best properties.

It is still living, what there is of it. The Nelson share intact and patient. Zami never parted with the Thembu half, now twenty-eight years old. Zami took it to Johannesburg, then to Orlando, Soweto, back to Johannesburg. Then to Capetown. Soweto. The traveling was incessant and perilous. The cake didn't suffer. When Zami was in prison, Zeni and Zindzi kept it and didn't touch it. The cake was their father, little brother, and baby. But then came the night of May 18, 1977, bang bang bang bang, and the cake suddenly cracked. By constantly holding out against persecution and constantly holding on, and being persecuted and saying no, being thrown in jail and forbidden to speak to three people . . . two people . . . one person, from going out after eight P.M. . . . seven P.M. . . . six P.M. . . . five P.M., forbidden to accompany Zindzi to school and forbidden to go into a shop to buy bread and to receive Reverend Father Rakale under her roof, and forbidden to enter a church and to go into any human construction, and from taking a road, from going by car, by bus, by train, by plane.

and by constantly not having touched an inch of Nelson's skin in thirteen years

suddenly on May 18, 1977, armed men came at four o'clock in the morning to seize her

when they raided her house in Orlando, and when they threw her and Zindzi in a truck and deported her to Brandfort,

that day the crumbling of the cake began. At the moment when Zami and Zindzi were thrown like garbage into a hut filled with refuse.

There was Zami lying helpless in the dust, her face stuck to the wretched skin of Africa, face to face with this land of pain, her lips on the maternal leprosy, and news of the crime went rumbling off, misery rolled over the large, humiliated, imploring body of Africa, misery with its army, trucks, machine guns, vacant eyes, its cadaverous cheeks and terrifying misery of idiocy, misery going off on its wheels gunning its motors in the sad African silence, then news of the crime died out, the poor night fell trembling back over its rags and its godforsaken children, and there was Zindzi, clinging to Zami with all her hands, her dozens of anguished little arms, like ten desperate children, like the little girl who can take no more of the universe and strikes her mother's belly and would like to go back in, clinging as only human children do who hope to scale walls and cross borders and flee life by way of love. And had Zami been able to open and take Zindzi back into the uterine nest, oh what relief for a share of her pain.

The silence fell on her like a blanket of tears.

Then Zami's body cracked, the earth cracked, and from its central core all the world's outrage collected into lava of blood trying to spurt up to the sky, to the impassive face of God, to God's untearful eyes and here with all her might, from every sinew of her body, Zami hurled a long powerful heart-rending wail at God's deafness!

And in that Brandfort night there was absolutely no one.

Only the cake heard and for the first time it broke. The cake was going to turn thirteen.

But in the end the cake had the best of it. The dough proved stronger than all the forces of decomposition and dispersion. Not a crumb was lost. Zami saved them all.

Today the cake is twenty-eight. All the crumbs are in safe-keeping in Orlando. Nelson has been in Pollsmoor Prison in Capetown since April 1982. I am writing this in April 1986. All the Mandela crumbs are living.

What is a twenty-eight-year-old cake? What will its flesh taste like when Nelson and Zami finish marrying?

The taste of earth flowing with the milk and honey of Zami's tears.

▲　▲

On Friday, June 12, 1964, Nelson Mandela was sentenced never in his life to spend a merciful human hour in Winnie Mandela's arms.

On Friday, June 12, 1964, Nelson and Winnie were sentenced to have love's body cut and separated into two parts forever quivering, forever thirsty, forever dying without dying, forever hoping without hope.

At this moment, when I am feeling in my body the cruel hunger of bodies ceaselessly wanting and wanting and not having, it is raining. Sometimes it rains, doing this anguished land a little good. And I too weep.

And before June 12, 1964, there was November 7, 1962. And before November 7, 1962, there was March 21, 1960, and before the day in Sharpeville and before and before there was December 1952, and before the trial for treason there was 1948, and before the infamous apartheid laws there were so many befores. And Nelson was born July 18, 1919. And afterward there was Wednesday, June 16, 1976. And after the day of Soweto, there was September 1977. And after the death of Steve Biko, there had been . . .

The soul can be taught patiences, the sublime accounts: "Time transforms each prison day to glory. Time with subtle phrases will turn your mortal pains to eternal honor. Your tears turn to pearls. The black, gold, and green of your country's flag is cut from your noble skin. Nothing of this destructive destiny but the waves of History change into such strange splendor."

But the body understands no patience. In the Mandela passion the bodies are dying alive. For he is a man, she a woman. And because in addition to feeling like a man and a woman one in front of the other, he is a handsome man and she a beautiful woman.

Then, nearly every day from June 12, 1964, on, they struggle, they run in place toward each other, they do not fall into each other's arms, they do not fondle the velvet breast with a joyous hand, they do not taste each other, they desire each other and ruin themselves and die one of two deaths, for the nursing body separated from the nutritive body escapes torture by fire only to fall into the freezing abyss.

They go from worse to worse. There's the devil's genius: making the worst worse.

The separation increases inventions. The worst prisons are added. The prison spreads like the plague. Nelson's prison imprisons Winnie, Zindzi, Zeni. Nelson in prison in penal servitude at Robben Island must live Winnie in prison in 1967, in 1969, in 1970, in 1976, in 1977, in. It is then that he is truly in prison.

What lessens my suffering is your suffering.

What increases my suffering is your suffering.

I suffer from you suffering. The one and the other, they force themselves to smile.

Without sex, without arms, without nose, without hands, without bread, without honeycake. And eyes?

It has come to nourishment of the eyes when Zami goes to see Nelson, finally after six months, after a year, after two years without everything:

In the half-light, through the cruelly thick glass, the hazy sight of Nelson's head to the exclusion of his body. She doesn't see his hair, she doesn't see his forehead, nor his eyes, nor his smile. And his voice? She doesn't hear his voice. Through the pitiless earphones comes a voice without color or timbre. In a voiceless voice Nelson speaks, the father of her children, "How are my people? Tell them it won't be long and that I am with them."

Could this be true? It could be true.

"Time's up!"

She didn't see him. She didn't hear him. Twelve years without touching his skin. And yet there he was. She didn't inhale the aroma of this tall handsome desirable indomitable man. And yet here she was. This was a marvelous visit. In 1981 he recomposed for her a sentence about the body she could no longer live in. How attractive you are, my darling, my black dove, earrings down to your breasts like your lover's fingers, my fingers. And then what happens between Nelson and Zami, and between their bodies only a shadow of which the glass lets through, one for the other? A marriage. One of their marriages, that's what happens.

The secret of Nelson's strength. He was a born maternal father. And yet Winnie is his mother, and his daughter.

One of Winnie's secrets: how she perfumes herself before seeing Nelson.

Nelson's courage is to summon up courage when there's no more courage. And where to look for it? Ask the mice scurrying through the cell how they do it. When he feels hope has gone, he gets up and goes to clean the toilet bucket of his cellmate Daniels. And he finds courage at the bottom of the bucket.

After all these years-centuries of silence and confinement, he believes that on the outside in the country where time goes by like the wind blowing away events, the people think of him every day. Twenty years have passed since his last public words. He still believes that no one has forgotten him. How does he do it? He thinks of the people every day, forgetting no one.

But how is it that this belief doesn't wither away?

I don't know. It's love. It's a miracle.

For twenty-five years Mandela has been the name most uttered in the South African air.

And all the things Winnie didn't know as a little girl, when the races by the river and the beauty of the verdant hills led her to believe the world was hers, all the strange secrets no one had spoken of, she discovered through the prison and the separation.

That so many agonies added to so many angers and so many regrets and so many thousands and thousands of exhaustions and despairs, this can end up producing something good.

For twelve years I haven't seen your legs.

This year of 1982 I saw your whole body down to the waist.

This year of 1983 I saw through the glass your whole left foot.

What do they give you to eat? Since June 12, 1964, I haven't known what your mouth has tasted.

I think of these three tomato plants as my own children.

Pains = Riches.

In India, too, one achieves immortalities after five hundred years of fasting.

But this hellish bodily torment, this rack of innocents, Winnie, Nelson cannot want it to cease, one can hope only to suffer it again and again, for it is cut from the ever-living desire. This torment is the wail of the exiled body's delight.

> "May the prison not close in on my desire. My body's soul remains free. May I suffer in my arms and in my breast and down to the soles of my feet from the same unbearable hunger. May I believe I shall die of pain at each visit, before and during and after, in twenty years and in thirty years and when my hair will be white, and my face worn. Give us the daily biting hunger, grant us no distraction, keep us to the end of all assuagement. Amen."
>
> Almandela! Nwagethu!

Mandela. Almandela. In the bitter and inedible shell, the almond is tender, like the flesh of the first little child. The almond is there, beneath the bitterness. That is the secret of Mandela.

Is there another secret?

The tender hope in hopeless.

Happy are those whose cause is absolutely just.

Some causes are absolutely pure. There is at least one. May it stay that way.

The first part of the royal cake made with African almonds was blessed and consummated in June 1958, at Bizana in Pondoland.

The second part will be eaten in 19__ in Qunu in the region of Umtata, down to the last crumb.

And all this martyrdom will have been a long and painful marriage ceremony.

The marriage of a people with its land.

Translated from the French by Franklin Philip

JOYCE
CAROL OATES

▼▼

FOR NELSON MANDELA

▼

Apartheid is one of the enduring shadows of evil of our time. It falls upon those of us who enjoy political freedom and severely qualifies that freedom, just as this century's unique campaigns against life—the Holocaust, the proliferation of nuclear arms—severely qualify our personal hopes, ambitions, and dreams of happiness. Of apartheid's peculiar evil Nelson Mandela has long been the symbol of heroic, living resistance. How beyond the confines, even the eloquence, of any poetry, this man's achievement!

Yet in contemplating apartheid as symbol in itself the writer is led to contemplate the ongoing tragedy of mankind's historical madness. The split in the self yields a split in the community of selves: the inner shadow falling upon the outer world, with disastrous consequences for the disenfranchised. Warring twins, brother-selves, "white" and "black" so forced into an artificial contention—it is not possible to imagine apartheid, as any aspect of tyranny, or genocide, without imagining too a kind of desire: the yearning for a wholeness that eludes us all. That which is despised, and denied, and rendered "mute" may become the very image, however unacknowledged, of desire.

Most writers are ambivalent about the political worth, in even the most modest, abstract terms, of work to which they have devoted their lives. What can art, however well intentioned, however ardent, do to alleviate the suffering of so many millions of enslaved men and women; or to suggest the heroism of an individual imprisoned, like Nelson Mandela, for more than two decades . . . ? The outsider, the witness, casts himself in the role of dreamer, or dream diviner. The vision is inevitably incomplete but it is a vision, of sorts, nonetheless.

DESIRE

⫢

All his life he has been lonely so naturally he marries often. Impregnates the women as quickly as possible then stands back, observing, to wait.

He loves the fat swelling bellies, the beautiful women staggering with their own weight as if deliciously drunk—that grip of a woman's fingers on his arm, the warm moist breath. He loves the heavy breasts filled to bursting, giving suck to drowsy babies, leaking milk on the pillow. He loves even the knowing that these lives depend so utterly upon *his*.

So he tells himself: I love.

Actually he gets bored fairly quickly. He tries for constancy, fidelity, the old honored virtues, but it doesn't work: that isn't his nature. A pang of desire strikes keen and sharp as a wire piercing his flesh and he knows he must move on and, well, he does move on . . . these matters can't be legislated after all.

The heart has its reasons, says Pascal. That reason knows not.

Or words to that effect.

All his life he has been lonely so naturally he seeks friendship . . . friends. Boys in school, men in his profession, the husbands of his wives' friends and in some cases the husbands of the women with whom he sleeps. Hello he says and shakes hands and his frank staring eyes seek out the other's in a plea

223

that is sometimes (he knows, to his shame) too direct, too raw. At other times it is all under control and the conversation springs up naturally, the swift happy coincidences of certain hobbies, sports, political beliefs, hopes. When he gets to know a man reasonably well and is certain the man will not betray him by violating his confidence he might tell him as if casually about his loneliness; his *mysterious* loneliness. (Is it shared? Is it even understood?) He has perhaps too frequently and too impulsively confessed that he'd always envied children with large families—older sisters, brothers—he'd observed them out of his particular aloneness as the only child of "older" parents and believed that, there, amid even the bickering and pummeling, *there* lay the secret of all happiness.

Only once, misinterpreting a friend's sympathy as an invitation to further intimacy, did he dare ask the man about *his* present circumstances. Was he happily married?—was he happy, being a father? Or did he too, from time to time, feel this strange inexplicable all-pervading loneliness?—the mere word inadequate to describe an emptiness ten times emptied, a void, a nullity, a vacuum from which all light, color, texture, substance, form has fled?

His friend looked at him sharply and he saw that the man was no friend. The answer came swiftly: Yes. Of course he was happy. Of course from time to time he felt "lonely"—briefly—who doesn't? But why is it important?

He thinks: how much harder to court another man, than any woman. How much more treacherous—dangerous. To a woman you can say, Shall we make love? Shall we get married? But to no man can you say, Shall we be friends? Shall we be—*brothers*?

For it's really a brother he wants, not a friend. Not a sister—his childhood fantasies never really involved sisters—just a brother! a single brother!

And his life, so unsatisfying, so curiously lacerated, would have been whole.

▲ ▲

There was a pretty young woman, one of his wives in fact, who chided him often for being so "morbid." For thinking about the kinds of things other people rarely thought about.

"Meaning—?"

"I don't know. Death, dying, that sort of thing. The purpose behind things, or what people do," she said carelessly. "I don't know. But I don't like it."

He asked the young woman pleasantly what were the things she believed he should think about, in that case.

"Me. Us. The baby."

"Well—of course I do."

"Do you?"

"I do."

"Yes but *do* you?"

He was beginning not to be charmed but he laughed and kissed her, for all things, with women, with *his* women, were resolved in kisses until such time as his desire died.

But he thought, She knows.

He thought, I haven't deceived this one.

What it was, however, that the young woman knew, and knew about him, he could not have named.

He blames his parents, he *was* an only child.

He blames his parents, they had him so very late it was almost *too* late.

A mother forty years older than he and a father fifty-two years older . . . He loved them but they weren't enough, not nearly enough, there was his white-haired father laughing when asked if the little boy was his grandchild, "No, he happens to be my son," while his mother stood stiff and indignant and said nothing at all.

There was the quiet house, the still house, the house that in his memory, is empty; waiting to be filled.

It isn't true of course that he blames his parents, he knows better. He's a reasonable man, an adult, no longer a child pining away in loneliness. He's a man with a "solid reputation" in his profession and he's a "success" you might say (he grants himself a moderate success, at least). And if he falls in love often, and marries often, and has fathered too many children, it's out of an excess feeling, an extravagant spiritual generosity—you might say.

"You're the most romantic man I know," a woman once told him. "You seem to have such faith."

"I do? Do I?" he'd asked excitedly. "Faith in what, do you think—?"

He begins to read voraciously in his spare time. And not always in his spare time, but at his desk, in secret, when he really ought to be attending to other things. Gilt-stamped luxury volumes of simulated leather smelling of newness, and antiquity—the "wisdom of the ages" from Plato to Wittgenstein. Or handsome paperback editions of classics that, in his time, were scorned by his generation as no longer relevant to theirs. Dickens, Swift, Shakespeare—of course—but it is Milton who most engages his imagination; and these lines from *Paradise Lost* that arouse in him a sympathy so intense he understands it is one of the secrets of his emotional life.

> I thither went
> With unexperienc't thought, and laid me down
> On the green bank, to look into the clear
> Smooth Lake, that to me seem'd another Sky.
> As I bent down to look, just opposite,
> A Shape within the watr'y gleam appear'd
> Bending to look on me, I started back,
> It started back, but pleas'd I soon return'd,
> Pleas'd it return'd as soon with answering looks
> Of sympathy and love; and there I had fixt
> Mine eyes till now, and pin'd with vain desire.

By the time he is fifty-seven years old he has married four times, is responsible for the financial upkeep of several households, yet he falls in love again—again!—and marries again, a woman already pregnant with his child. When the baby is born this will be how many children?—six? seven? And his young wife will very likely want another.

"I'm greedy," she says. "Like you."

And then one day he learns that he has a tumorous growth in his colon that must be removed; and is removed; and is discovered to be benign. But during the course of the operation the surgeon discovers another growth in his lower abdomen—the mummified remains, weighing scarcely an ounce, of what was to have been his twin.

His twin!

Such things happen, sometimes, his doctor tells him. Of course it's highly unusual—monozygotic or "identical" twins are in themselves highly unusual—and in these rare cases it happens that one fetus drains blood and oxygen from the other and gradually overpowers it, kills it, absorbs it into his body. And at the time of his birth, long before today's medical technology, no one knew, of course, that there had ever been another fetus in his mother's womb.

"Then I was meant to have a twin?—to be a twin?" he asks, astonished.

"Evidently not," says his doctor. "Considering the evidence."

Smiling, he weighs the thing in the palm of his hand.

He contemplates it, pokes it with a finger: tough little calcified rubber knob, a wizened plum, just—nothing. You'd never guess what it is or from where it was taken and you'd never be able to tell from looking at it, peering at it under the desk lamp, whether it's something to laugh over, or mourn. Sometimes, staring at it, he can't control his laughter—tears streak his face. His twin! His! Fifty-seven years later! Other times, he's mute with grief. Sits unmoving just staring transfixed at the thing in the palm of his hand that, weightless, weighs so much.

"So this is it," he says.

▲   ▲

His wife says, "You wouldn't be so unhappy if you thought about other people for a change, instead of always—whatever it is you think about."

He says pleasantly, "What *is* it, do you imagine, that I think about?—that I shouldn't, I mean, think about."

"I don't know," she says evenly. "I don't know but I don't like it. It's just something I sense."

She's twenty-six years younger than he and knows she will outlive him. Or walk away from him when it's time—the first of his wives to do so.

Carefully he asks, "What should I think about, then?"

"Me. Us. The new baby. Your other children."

"But I do. I think about you all the time."

"Do you?" she asks skeptically.

"Of course," he says smiling. "What else is there, after all, to think about?"

JOHN
IRVING

WHEN A COUNTRY SO GROSSLY MISTREATS ITS CITIZENS, IT HEAPS SHAME UPON ITSELF

 ▼▼

More than five years ago, *The New York Times* invited me to write an essay for a series the *Book Review* was featuring, called "The Making of a Writer." It was a pleasant assignment. I remember thinking, at the time, that it was a luxury to indulge myself in this recollection, which is of a most free and interior kind. Ideally, in a free society, a writer is afforded this luxury—to freely imagine even the reconstruction of his own autobiography; and to search his own mind's interior, without society's interference.

Reading this little essay today, in the light of the South African situation, I am struck by how fragile and personal a memoir it seems; were I a South African writer, the subject of my writing would necessarily have to be the country itself—its monstrous interference with the freedoms and rights of its citizens, its cruel indifference to its citizens' misery.

Of course, this little essay also notices the mistreatment of a citizen; but how free the writer's eye is—to notice other things. Were I a South African writer, I would not have had the luxury to write like this. When a country so grossly mistreats its citizens, it heaps shame upon itself; and the writer can reflect upon only the shame.

TRYING TO SAVE
PIGGY SNEED

This is a memoir, but please understand that (to any writer with a good imagination) all memoirs are false. A fiction writer's memory is an especially imperfect provider of detail; we can always imagine a better detail than the one we can remember. The correct detail is rarely, exactly, what happened; the most truthful detail is what *could* have happened, or what *should* have. Half my life is an act of revision; more than half the act is performed with small changes. Being a writer is a strenuous marriage between careful observation and just as carefully imagining the truths you haven't had the opportunity to see. The rest is the necessary, strict toiling with the language; for me this means writing and rewriting the sentences until they sound as spontaneous as good conversation.

With that in mind, I think that I have become a writer because of my grandmother's good manners and—more specifically—because of a retarded garbage collector to whom my grandmother was always polite and kind.

My grandmother is the oldest living English literature major to have graduated from Wellesley. She lives in an old people's home, now, and her memory is fading; she doesn't remember the garbage collector who helped me become a writer, but she has retained her good manners and her kindness. When other old people wander into her room, by mistake—looking for their own rooms, or perhaps for their previous residences—my grandmother always says, "Are you lost, dear? Can I help you find where you're *supposed* to be?"

I lived with my grandmother, in her house, until I was almost seven; for this reason, my grandmother has always called me "her boy." In fact, she never had a boy of her own; she has three daughters. Whenever I have to say good-bye to her, now, we both know she might not live for another visit, and she always says, "Come back soon, dear. You're *my boy,* you know"—insisting, quite properly, that she is more than a grandmother to me.

Despite her being an English literature major, she has not read my work with much pleasure; in fact, she read my first novel and stopped (for life) with that. She disapproved of the language and the subject matter, she told me; from what she's read about the others, she's learned that my language and my subject matter utterly degenerate as my work matures. She's made no effort to read the four novels that followed the first (she and I agree this is for the best). She's very proud of me, she says; I've never probed too deeply concerning *what* she's proud of me *for*—for growing up, at all, perhaps, or just for being "her boy"—but she's certainly never made me feel uninteresting or unloved.

I grew up on Front Street in Exeter, New Hampshire. When I was a boy, Front Street was lined with elms; it wasn't Dutch elm disease that killed most of them. The two hurricanes that struck back to back, in the fifties, wiped out the elms and strangely modernized the street. First Carol came and weakened their roots; then Edna came and knocked them down. My grandmother used to tease me by saying that she hoped this would contribute to my respect for women.

When I was a boy, Front Street was a dark, cool street— even in the summer—and none of the backyards was fenced; everyone's dog ran free, and got into trouble. A man named Poggio delivered groceries to my grandmother's house. A man named Strout delivered the ice for the icebox (my grandmother resisted refrigerators until the very end). Mr. Strout was unpopular with the neighborhood dogs—perhaps because he would go after them with the ice tongs. We children of Front Street never bothered Mr. Poggio, because he used to let us hang around his store—and he was liberal with treats. We never bothered Mr. Strout, either (because of his ice tongs and his fabulous aggression toward dogs, which we could easily imagine being turned toward us). But the garbage collector had nothing for us—no treats, no aggression—and so we children reserved our capacity for teasing and taunting (and otherwise making trouble) for him.

His name was Piggy Sneed. He smelled worse than any man I *ever* smelled—with the possible exception of a dead man I caught the scent of, once, in Istanbul. And you would have to be dead to look worse than Piggy Sneed looked to us children on Front Street. There were so many reasons for calling him "Piggy," I wonder why one of us didn't think of a more original name. To begin with, he lived on a pig farm. He raised pigs, he slaughtered pigs; more importantly, he lived *with* his pigs—it was *just* a pig farm, there was no farm house, there was *only* the barn. There was a single stovepipe running into one of the stalls. That stall was heated by a wood stove for Piggy Sneed's comfort—and, we children imagined, his pigs (in the winter) would crowd around him for warmth. He certainly smelled that way.

Also he had absorbed, by the uniqueness of his retardation and by his proximity to his animal friends, certain piglike expressions and gestures. His face would jut in front of his body when he approached the garbage cans, as if he were rooting (hungrily) underground; he squinted his small, red eyes; his nose twitched with all the vigor of a snout; there were deep pink wrinkles on the back of his neck—and the pale bristles, which sprouted at random along his jawline, in no way resembled a beard. He was short, heavy, and strong—he *heaved* the garbage cans to his back, he *hurled* their contents into the wooden, slat-sided truck bed. In the truck, ever eager to receive the garbage, there were always a few pigs. Perhaps he took different pigs with him on different days; perhaps it was a treat for them—they didn't have to wait to eat the gar-

bage until Piggy Sneed drove it home. He took *only* garbage—
no paper, plastic, or metal trash—and it was *all* for his pigs.
This was all he did; he had a very exclusive line of work. He
was paid to pick up garbage, which he fed to his pigs. When
he got hungry (we imagined), he ate a pig. "A whole pig, at
once," we used to say on Front Street. But the *piggiest* thing
about him was that he couldn't talk. His retardation either
had deprived him of his human speech or had deprived him,
earlier, of the ability to learn human speech. Piggy Sneed didn't
talk. He grunted. He squealed. He *oinked*—that was his language; he learned it from his friends, as we learn ours.

We children, on Front Street, would sneak up on him when
he was raining the garbage down on his pigs—we'd surprise
him: from behind hedges, from under porches, from behind
parked cars, from out of garages and cellar bulkheads. We'd
leap out at him (we never got too close) and we'd squeal at
him: "Piggy! Piggy! Piggy! Piggy! OINK! WEEEE!" And, like a
pig—panicked, lurching at random, mindlessly startled (*every
time* he was startled, as if he had no memory)—Piggy Sneed
would squeal back at us as if we'd stuck him with the slaugh-
tering knife, he'd bellow OINK! out at us as if he'd caught us
trying to bleed him in his sleep.

I can't imitate his sound; it was awful, it made all us Front
Street children scream and run and hide. When the terror
passed, we couldn't wait for him to come again. He came
twice a week. What a luxury! And every week or so my grandmother would pay him. She'd come out to the back where his
truck was—where we'd often just startled him and left him
snorting—and she'd say, "Good day, Mr. Sneed!"

Piggy Sneed would become instantly childlike—falsely busy,
painfully shy, excruciatingly awkward. Once he hid his face
in his hands, but his hands were covered with coffee grounds;
once he crossed his legs so suddenly, while he tried to turn
his face away from Grandmother, that he fell down at her
feet.

"It's nice to see you, Mr. Sneed," Grandmother would say—
not flinching, not in the slightest, from his stench. "I hope

the children aren't being rude to you," she'd say. "You don't have to tolerate any rudeness from them, you know," she would add. And then she'd pay him his money and peer through the wooden slats of the truck bed, where his pigs were savagely attacking the new garbage—and, occasionally, each other—and she'd say, "What beautiful pigs these are! Are these your *own* pigs, Mr. Sneed? Are they *new* pigs? Are these the same pigs as the other week?" But despite her enthusiasm for his pigs, she could never entice Piggy Sneed to answer her. He would stumble, and trip, and twist his way around her, barely able to contain his pleasure: that my grandmother clearly approved of his pigs, that she even appeared to approve (wholeheartedly!) of *him*. He would grunt softly to her.

When she'd go back in the house, of course—when Piggy Sneed would begin to back his ripe truck out the driveway— we Front Street children would surprise him again, popping up on both sides of the truck, making both Piggy and his pigs squeal in alarm, and snort with protective rage.

"Piggy! Piggy! Piggy! Piggy! OINK! WEEEE!"

He lived in Stratham—on a road out of our town that ran to the ocean, about eight miles away. I moved (with my father and mother) out of Grandmother's house (before I was seven, as I told you). Because my father was a teacher, we moved into academy housing—Exeter was an all-boys' school, then— and so our garbage (together with our nonorganic trash) was picked up by the school.

Now I would like to say that I grew older and realized (with regret) the cruelty of children, and that I joined some civic organization dedicated to caring for people like Piggy Sneed. I can't claim that. The code of small towns is simple but encompassing: if many forms of craziness are allowed, many forms of cruelty are ignored. Piggy Sneed was tolerated; he went on being himself, living like a pig. He was tolerated as a harmless animal is tolerated—by children, he was indulged; he was even encouraged to be a pig.

Of course, growing older, we Front Street children knew

that he was retarded—and gradually we learned that he drank a bit. The slat-sided truck, reeking of pig, of waste, or *worse* than waste, careened through town all the years I was growing up. It was permitted, it was given room to spill over—en route to Stratham. Now there was a town, Stratham! In small-town life is there anything more provincial than the tendency to sneer at *smaller* towns? Stratham was not Exeter (not that Exeter was much).

In Robertson Davies's novel *Fifth Business,* he writes about the townspeople of Deptford: "We were serious people, missing nothing in our community and feeling ourselves in no way inferior to larger places. We did, however, look with pitying amusement on Bowles Corners, four miles distant and with a population of one hundred and fifty. To live in Bowles Corners, we felt, was to be rustic beyond redemption."

Stratham was Bowles Corners to us Front Street children—it was "rustic beyond redemption." When I was fifteen, and began my association with the academy—where there were students from abroad, from New York, even from California—I felt so superior to Stratham that it surprises me, now, that I joined the Stratham Volunteer Fire Department; I don't remember *how* I joined. I think I remember that there was no Exeter Volunteer Fire Department; Exeter had the other kind of fire department, I guess. There were several Exeter residents—apparently in need of something to volunteer *for*?—who joined the Stratham Volunteers. Perhaps our contempt for the people of Stratham was so vast that we believed they could not even be relied upon to properly put out their own fires.

There was also an undeniable thrill, midst the routine rigors of prep-school life, to be a part of something that could call upon one's services without the slightest warning: that burglar alarm in the heart, which is the late-night ringing telephone—that call to danger, like a doctor's beeper shocking the orderly solitude and safety of the squash court. It made us Front Street children important; and, as we grew only slightly older, it gave us a status that only disasters can create for the young.

In my years as a firefighter, I never rescued anyone—I never even rescued anyone's pet. I never inhaled smoke, I never suffered a burn, I never saw a soul fall beyond the reach of the safety bag. Forest fires are the worst and I was only in one, and only on the periphery. My only injury—"in action"— was caused by a fellow firefighter throwing his Indian pump into a storage room where I was trying to locate my baseball cap. The pump hit me in the face and I had a bloody nose for about three minutes.

There were occasional fires of some magnitude at Hampton Beach (one night an unemployed saxophone player, reportedly wearing a pink tuxedo, tried to burn down the casino), but we were always called to the big fires as the last measure. When there was an eight- or ten-alarm fire, Stratham seemed to be called last; it was more an invitation to the spectacle than a call to arms. And the local fires in Stratham were either mistakes or lost causes. One night Mr. Skully, the meter reader, set his station wagon on fire by pouring vodka in the carburetor—because, he said, the car wouldn't start. One night Grant's dairy barn was ablaze, but all the cows—and even most of the hay—had been rescued before we arrived. There was nothing to do but let the barn burn, and hose it down so that cinders from it wouldn't catch the adjacent farm house on fire.

But the boots, the heavy hard hat (with your own number), the glossy black slicker—*your own ax!*—these were pleasures because they represented a kind of adult responsibility in a world where we were considered (still) too young to drink. And one night, when I was sixteen, I rode a hook-and-ladder truck out the coast road, chasing down a fire in a summer house near the beach (which turned out to be the result of children detonating a lawn mower with barbecue fluid), and there—weaving on the road in his stinking pick-up, blocking our importance, as independent of civic responsibility (or any other kind) as any pig—was a drunk-driving Piggy Sneed, heading home with his garbage for his big-eating friends.

We gave him the lights, we gave him the siren—I wonder,

now, what he thought was behind him. God, the red-eyed screaming monster over Piggy Sneed's shoulder—the great robot pig of the universe and outer space! Poor Piggy Sneed, near home, so drunk and foul as to be barely human, veered off the road to let us pass, and as we overtook him—we Front Street children—I distinctly heard us calling, "Piggy! Piggy! Piggy! Piggy! OINK! WEEEE!" I suppose I heard my voice, too.

Clinging to the hook-and-ladder, our heads thrown back so that the trees above the narrow road appeared to veil the stars with a black, moving lace—the pig smell faded to the raw, fuel-burning stink of the sabotaged lawn mower, which faded finally to the clean salt wind off the sea.

In the dark, driving back, past the pig barn, we noted the surprisingly warm glow from the kerosene lamp in Piggy Sneed's stall. He had gotten safely home. And was he up, reading? we wondered. And once again I heard our grunts, our squeals, our oinks—our strictly animal communication with him.

The night his pig barn burned, we were so surprised.

The Stratham Volunteers were used to thinking of Piggy Sneed's place as a necessary, reeking ruin on the road between Exeter and the beach—a foul-smelling landmark on warm summer evenings, passing it always engendered the obligatory groans. In winter, the smoke from the wood stove pumped regularly from the pipe above Piggy's stall, and from the outdoor pens, stamping routinely in a wallow of beshitted snow, his pigs breathed in little puffs as if they were furnaces of flesh. A blast from the siren could scatter them. At night, coming home, when whatever fire there was was out, we couldn't resist hitting the siren when we passed by Piggy Sneed's place. It was too exciting to imagine the damage done by that sound: the panic among the pigs, Piggy himself in a panic, all of them hipping up to each other with their wheezy squeals, seeking the protection of the herd.

The night Piggy Sneed's place burned, we Front Street children were imagining a larkish, if somewhat retarded, spectacle. Out the coast road, lights up full and flashing, siren up high—driving all those pigs crazy—we were in high spirits, telling lots of pig jokes: about how we imagined the fire was started, how they'd been having a drinking party, Piggy *and* his pigs, and Piggy was cooking one (on a spit) and dancing with another one, and some pig backed into the wood stove and burned his tail, knocked over the bar, and the pig that Piggy danced with *most* nights was ill-humored because Piggy *wasn't* dancing with *her* . . . but then we arrived, and we saw that this fire wasn't a party; it wasn't even the tail end of a bad party. It was the biggest fire that we Front Street children, and even the veterans among the Stratham Volunteers, had ever seen.

The low, adjoining sheds of the pig barn appeared to have burst, or melted their tin roofs. There was nothing in the barn that wouldn't burn—there was wood for the wood stove, there was hay, there were eighteen pigs and Piggy Sneed. There was all that kerosene. Most of the stalls in the pig barn were a couple of feet deep in manure, too. As one of the veterans of the Stratham Volunteers told me, "You get it hot enough, even shit will burn."

It was hot enough. We had to move the fire trucks down the road; we were afraid the new paint, or the new tires, would blister in the heat. "No point in wasting the water," our captain told us. We sprayed the trees across the road; we sprayed the woods beyond the pig barn. It was a windless, bitter cold night, the snow as dry and fine as talcum powder. The trees drooped with icicles and cracked as soon as we sprayed them. The captain decided to let the fire burn itself out; there would be less of a mess that way. It might be dramatic to say that we heard squeals, to say that we heard the pigs' intestines swelling and exploding—or before that, their hooves hammering on the stall doors. But by the time we arrived, those sounds were over; they were history; we could only imagine them.

This is a writer's lesson: to learn that the sounds we imagine can be the clearest, loudest sounds of all. By the time we arrived, even the tires on Piggy's truck had burst, the gas tank had exploded, the windshield had caved in. Since we hadn't been present for those events, we could only guess at the order in which they had taken place.

If you stood too close to the pig barn, the heat curled your eyelashes—the fluid under your eyelids felt searing hot. If you stood too far back, the chill of the winter night air, drawn toward the flames, would cut through you. The coast road iced over, because of spillage from our hoses, and (about midnight) a man with a Texaco emblem on his cap and parka skidded off the road and needed assistance. He was drunk and was with a woman who looked much too young for him—or perhaps it was his daughter. "Piggy!" the Texaco man hollered. "Piggy!" he called, into the blaze. "If you're in there, Piggy—you *moron*—you better get the hell out!"

The only other sound, until about two in the morning, was the occasional *twang* from the tin roof contorting—as it writhed free of the barn. About two the roof fell in; it made a whispering noise. By three there were no walls standing. The surrounding, melted snow had formed a lake that seemed to be rising on all sides of the fire, almost reaching the level of heaped coals. As more snow melted, the fire was being extinguished from underneath itself.

And what did we smell? That cooked-barnyard smell of midsummer, the conflicting rankness of ashes in snow, the determined baking of manure—the imagination of bacon, or roast pork. Since there was no wind, and we weren't trying to put the fire out, we suffered no smoke abuse. The men (that is to say, the veterans) left us boys to watch after things for an hour before dawn. That is what men do when they share work with boys: they do what they want to do, they have the boys tend to what they don't want to tend to. The men went out for coffee, they said, but they came back smelling of beer. By then the fire was low enough to be doused down. The men initiated this procedure; when they tired of it, they turned it over to us boys. The men went off again, at first light—for breakfast, they said. In the light I could recognize a few of my comrades, the Front Street children.

With the men away, one of the Front Street children started it—at first, very softly. It may have been me. "Piggy, Piggy," one of us called. One reason I'm a writer is that I sympathized with our need to do this; I have never been interested in what nonwriters call good and bad "taste."

"Piggy! Piggy! Piggy! Piggy! OINK! WEEEE!" we called. That was when I understood that comedy was just another form of condolence. And then I started it; I began my first story.

"Shit," I said—because everyone in the Stratham Volunteers began every sentence with the word "shit."

"Shit," I said. "Piggy Sneed isn't in there. He's crazy," I added, "but nobody's that stupid."

"His truck's there," said one of the least imaginative of the Front Street children.

"He just got sick of pigs," I said. "He left town, I know it. He was sick of the whole thing. He probably planned this—for weeks."

Miraculously, I had their attention. Admittedly, it had been a long night. *Anyone* with almost *anything* to say might have easily captured the attention of the Stratham Volunteers. But I felt the thrill of a rescue coming—my first.

"I bet there's not a pig in there, either," I said. "I bet he ate half of them—in just a few days. You know, he stuffed himself! And then he sold the rest. He's been putting some money away, for precisely this occasion."

"For *what* occasion? " some skeptic asked me. "If Piggy isn't in there, where is he?"

"If he's been out all night," another said, "then he's *frozen* to death."

"He's in Florida," I said. "He's retired." I said it just that simply—I said it as if it were a *fact*. "Look around you!" I shouted to them. "What's he been spending his money on? He's saved a bundle. He set fire to his own place," I said, "just to give us a hard time. Think of the hard time we gave him," I said, and I could see everyone thinking about that; that was, at least, the truth. A little truth never hurt a story. "Well," I concluded. "He's paid us back—that's clear. He's kept us standing around all night."

This made us Front Street children thoughtful, and in that thoughtful moment I started my first act of revision; I tried to make the story better, and more believable. It was essential to rescue Piggy Sneed, of course, but what would a man who couldn't talk do in *Florida*? I imagined they had tougher zoning laws than we had in New Hampshire—especially regarding pigs.

"You know," I said, "I bet he *could* talk—all the time. He's probably *European,*" I decided. "I mean, what kind of name is *Sneed*? And he first appeared here around the war, didn't he? Whatever his native language is, anyway, I bet he speaks it pretty well. He just never learned *ours*. Somehow, pigs were easier. Maybe *friendlier,*" I added, thinking of us all. "And now he's saved up enough to go home. That's where he is!" I said. "Not Florida—he's gone back to *Europe!*"

" 'Atta boy, Piggy," someone cheered.

"Look out, Europe," someone said, facetiously.

Enviously, we imagined how Piggy Sneed had gotten "out"—how he'd escaped the harrowing small-town loneliness (and fantasies) that threatened us all. But when the men came back, I was confronted with the general public's dubious regard for fiction.

"Irving thinks Piggy Sneed is in Europe," one of the Front Street boys told the captain.

"He first appeared here around the war, didn't he, sir?" I asked the captain, who was staring at me as if I were the first *body* to be recovered from this fire.

"Piggy Sneed was *born* here, Irving," the captain told me. "His mother was a half-wit, she got hit by a car going the wrong way around the bandstand. Piggy was born on Water Street," the captain told us. Water Street, I knew perfectly well, ran into Front Street—quite close to home.

So, I thought, Piggy was in Florida, after all. In stories, you must make the best thing that *can* happen happen (or the worst, if that is your aim), but it still has to ring true.

When the coals were cool enough to walk on, the men started looking for him; discovery was a job for the men—it being more interesting than waiting, which was boys' work.

After a while, the captain called me over to him. "Irving," he said. "Since you think Piggy Sneed is in Europe, then you won't mind taking whatever *this* is out of here."

It required little effort, the removal of this shrunken cinder of a man; I doused down a tarp and dragged the body, which was extraordinarily light, onto the tarp with first the long and then the short gaff. We found all eighteen of his pigs, too. But even today I can imagine him more vividly in Florida than I can imagine him existing in that impossibly small shape of charcoal I extricated from the ashes.

Of course I told my grandmother the *plain* truth, just the boring facts. "Piggy Sneed died in that fire last night, Nana," I told her.

"Poor Mr. Sneed," she said. With great wonder, and sympathy, she added: "What awful circumstances forced him to live such a savage life!"

What I would realize, later, is that the writer's business is *both* to imagine the possible rescue of Piggy Sneed *and* to set the fire that will trap him. It was *much* later—but before my grandmother was moved to the old people's home, when she still remembered who Piggy Sneed was—when Grandmother asked me, "Why, in heaven's name, have you become a *writer?*"

I was "her boy," as I've told you, and she was sincerely worried about me. Perhaps being an English literature major had convinced her that being a writer was a lawless and destructive thing to be. And so I told her everything about the night of the fire, about how I imagined that if I could have invented well enough—if I could have made up something truthful enough—that I could have (in some sense) saved Piggy Sneed. At least saved him for another fire—of my own making.

Well, my grandmother is a Yankee—*and* Wellesley's oldest

living English literature major. Fancy answers, especially of an aesthetic nature, are not for her. Her late husband—my grandfather—was in the shoe business; he made things people really needed: practical protection for their feet. Even so, I insisted to Grandmother that her kindness to Piggy Sneed had not been overlooked by me—and that this, in combination with the helplessness of Piggy Sneed's special human condition, and the night of the fire, which had introduced me to the possible power of my own imagination . . . and so forth. My grandmother cut me off.

With more pity than vexation, she patted my hand, she shook her head. "Johnny, *dear*," she said. "You surely could have saved yourself a lot of *bother*, if you'd only treated Mr. Sneed with a little human decency when he was alive."

Failing that, I realize that a writer's business is setting fire to Piggy Sneed—*and* trying to save him—again and again; forever.

MAURICE
BLANCHOT

▼

OUR RESPONSIBILITY

W

What is a fit way to speak and write about the segregation of whites and blacks? We see that what mankind experienced when the Nazis excluded a part of humanity from life and the right to life has survived the calamitous defeat that once seemed to make this wretched doctrine impossible, even unstatable.

As it happened, apartheid took legal form just as the colonialist nations were caving in from the realization that they had no exclusive right to personify the diversity of the human spirit. For the Afrikaners, the process happened in reverse, as though the onus was on them to halt development and to realize Hegel's ill-considered assertion that "Africa has no history." If one were looking for excuses, one might say that the Afrikaners have not changed, but have kept and even strengthened the old colonialist prejudices (of the sixteenth and seventeenth centuries at the time Montaigne discovered there were different yet equal cultures).

At the outset these adventurers, seeking to put down roots in unknown lands, had going for them their might, an exclusive culture, and a restricted and for that matter persecuted religion. Centuries went by. The outmoded imperatives remained in force, protected only by savage (and contradictory) regulations. It was understood, more or less implicitly, that coloreds and whites each had their own culture which could develop only in reciprocal separation. This hypocritical decision almost immediately yielded to the terror of numbers and the necessity of employing "inferiors" for menial work. Blacks and whites came into contact, an indispensable coexistence that had its dangers. In many cases the blacks had to be present (so as to work) and also not present (lacking the right to purely personal or idle presence).

This is how apartheid has produced a set of laws almost more unbearable than slavery. The blacks are indispensable, but expose the whites to dangerous contamination. Similarly, it is a great crime for the black to acquire Western-style culture. When an evil like this occurs, it upsets the social equilibrium and can lead to communism or something like it. Hence the conviction of Nelson Mandela. He is too educated and too capable to be allowed freedom. Communism, community, and democracy are precluded. Finally, laws are insufficient, for they contain certain guarantees. So they must be abrogated. It is a state of emergency, the prohibition of free information, a withdrawal into one's own world, and an eventual break with the rest of the world, except for commercial goods, trade being the final truth.

I am not summoning up these hard facts merely so that they will not fade from memory, but also so that the memory of them makes us more aware of our responsibility. We are a party to the barbarousness, the suffering, and the countless murders to the extent that we greet these facts with a certain indifference and spend our days and nights untroubled. It is striking that the man unfortunately serving as the French prime minister scoffs at what he calls our concern for a clear conscience—his own is assuredly unaffected by what is happening down there, in another world. Moreover, the European community's inertia does discredit to the ideals and civilization that community claims to represent. Let us realize, therefore, that we too are responsible and guilty when we do not voice an appeal, a denunciation, and a cry.

And let us be the kind of people who can repeat the words of Breyten Breytenbach, addressed to Winnie Mandela:

Our heart is with you.
Africa will be freed.

Translated from the French by Franklin Philip

BIOGRAPHICAL NOTES

▼

ADONIS: Adonis is a Lebanese poet. He writes in Arabic and French and has been published in France.

JORGE AMADO: Jorge Amado was born in 1912 in Bahia, Brazil, where he lives today. He is the author of *Dona Flor and Her Two Husbands* (Avon), *Sea of Death* (Avon), and *Showdown* (Bantam), among many other works.

JOHN ASHBERY: John Ashbery won the Pulitzer Prize, the National Book Award, and the National Book Critics Circle Award for his 1975 volume of poetry, *Self-Portrait in a Convex Mirror* (Penguin). He teaches creative writing at Brooklyn College of the City University of New York. A new collection of poems, *April Galleons,* will be published by Viking in October 1987.

SAMUEL BECKETT: Nobel Prize winner Samuel Beckett was born in Ireland, but since the 1920s he has made his home in France. His work includes drama (*Waiting for Godot, Endgame*), novels (*Molloy, Malone Dies, The Unnamable*), and short fiction (*The Lost Ones, Ill Seen Ill Said*).

OLYMPE BHÊLY-QUÊNUM: A citizen of Benin, Olympe Bhêly-Quênum lives in Paris and writes in French. Winner in 1966 of the Grand Prix Littéraire d'Afrique, he has published *Un Piège sans fin* (Stock), *Le Chant du lac* (Présence Africaine), *Un Enfant d'Afrique* (Larousse), and *L'Initié* (Présence Africaine).

MAURICE BLANCHOT: Maurice Blanchot was born on December 22, 1907. He is France's preeminent literary critic and the author

253

of fiction, as well. Among his works are *The Space of Literature* (University of Nebraska Press), *The Writing of Disaster* (University of Nebraska Press), and *Death Sentence* (Station Hill Press).

WILLIAM S. BURROUGHS: William S. Burroughs was born in St. Louis, Missouri, in 1914. One of the most peripatetic writers of the twentieth century, he has spent most of his life in Mexico, Tangiers, Paris, London, and South America. At present he lives in Kansas. His published works include *Naked Lunch* (Grove), *Cities of the Red Night* (Henry Holt), *The Last Words of Dutch Schultz* (Seaver), and *The Adding Machine* (Seaver).

HÉLÈNE CIXOUS: Born in Oran, Algeria, Hélène Cixous is a noted feminist and writer, and a professor of English literature at the Université de Paris, Vincennes. Her book *Newly Born Woman*, co-written with Catherine Clément, was published in 1986 by the University of Minnesota Press.

JACQUES DERRIDA: The philosopher Jacques Derrida was born in El Biar, Algeria, in 1930. He teaches at the Ecole des Hautes Etudes en Sciences Sociales in Paris and has held visiting professorships at eminent universities in the United States. Among his works are *Of Grammatology* (Johns Hopkins), *Dissemination* (University of Chicago Press), *Glas* (University of Nebraska Press), and *Memoires for Paul De Man* (Columbia University Press).

ALLEN GINSBERG: For decades a major voice in American poetry, Allen Ginsberg is currently a Distinguished Professor at Brooklyn College. His recent collections of poems, published by Harper & Row, include *Collected Poems, 1947–1980*, *White Shroud: Poems 1980–1985*, and *Howl*.

NADINE GORDIMER: Born in 1923, Nadine Gordimer has lived all her life in South Africa, where she has been an outspoken opponent of apartheid. Her ninth novel, *A Sport of Nature* (Knopf), was published this year. Her most recent book of short stories—her eighth—is *Something Out There* (Viking).

JUAN GOYTISOLO: Born in Barcelona, Spain, Juan Goytisolo fled Franco's repressive regime in 1957. He remained in exile after Franco's fall, and now divides his time among Paris, New York, and Marrakech. He is the author of acclaimed novels, including *Juan the Landless, Count Julian,* and *Makbara.* His *Landscapes After the Battle* was published in 1987 by Seaver Books.

RICHARD HOWARD: Richard Howard is a Pulitzer Prize–winning poet, critic, and translator. His next volume of poems, *No Traveler,* will be published in 1988.

JOHN IRVING: John Irving was born in Exeter, New Hampshire, in 1942. His first novel, *Setting Free the Bears* (Pocket Books), was published in 1968. He is also the author of *The Water Method Man* (Pocket Books), *The 158-Pound Marriage* (Pocket Books), *The World According to Garp* (Pocket Books), *The Hotel New Hampshire* (Pocket Books), and *The Cider House Rules* (Bantam).

EDMOND JABÈS: Poet Edmond Jabès was born in Cairo on April 14, 1912. He has lived in France since 1957. His *The Book of Questions* has been published by Wesleyan University Press.

DOMINIQUE LECOQ: Dominique Lecoq is the editor of the magazine *Aujourd'hui l'Afrique.*

MICHEL LEIRIS: Michel Leiris is a poet, novelist, art critic, and ethnologist, but his greatest influence in modern letters has been in his autobiographical works, beginning with *Manhood* (1939, available in English from North Point Press); the work continues in this vein with the four-part series *La Règle du jeu* (1948–1968).

HEINER MÜLLER: East Berliner Heiner Müller was born in 1929 in a small town in what used to be called Saxony. He is the author of *Hamletmachine and Other Texts for the Stage,* edited by Carl Weber (PAJ Publications).

JOYCE CAROL OATES: Joyce Carol Oates is the Roger S. Berlind Distinguished Lecturer in Creative Writing at Princeton University. Her book *ON BOXING* was recently published by Dolphin/Doubleday. Her most recent novel is *You Must Remember This,* published by Dutton.

SEVERO SARDUY: Cuban poet Severo Sarduy has published in this country *For Voice,* edited by Yvette E. Miller (Latin American Literary Review Press).

NTOZAKE SHANGE: Ntozake Shange is a playwright (*for colored girls who have considered suicide/ when the rainbow is enuf* and *Three Pieces*), poet (*nappy edges* and *A Daughter's Geography*), and novelist *(Sassafras, Cypress, & Indigo* and *Betsey Brown*) who publishes with St. Martin's Press. She lives in Houston, Texas.

SUSAN SONTAG: Susan Sontag's contribution first appeared, in French, in the original Gallimard volume *Pour Nelson Mandela*. Her most recent books are *I, etcetera* (stories) and *Under the Sign of Saturn* (essays). She is at work on a new novel, and Farrar, Straus & Giroux is bringing out a uniform paperback edition of her books.

MUSTAPHA TLILI: The Tunisian writer Mustapha Tlili lives in New York City and has published three novels with Gallimard, in Paris: *La Rage aux tripes, Le Bruit dort,* and *Gloire des sables.* In 1986 he was made Knight of the French Ordre des Arts et des Lettres.

KATEB YACINE: The Algerian novelist and playwright Kateb Yacine has published two novels with Seuil, in Paris—*Nedjma* and *Le Polygone étoilé*—and many plays, among which are *Le Cadavre encerclé* and *L'Homme aux sandales de caoutchouc.* His most recent work, *L'Oeuvre en fragments,* was published by Sindbad in 1986. He received the French Grand Prix National des Arts et des Lettres in 1987.